Battle on the Rosebush

Battle
on the Rosebush

Insect Life In Your Backyard

Marian S. Edsall
Illustrated by Jean Cassels Helmer

Follett Publishing Company/Chicago

J
595.7
E
c. 1

Acknowledgment is made to Dr. Roy D. Shenefelt of the
Department of Entomology, College of Agriculture and Life Sciences,
University of Wisconsin for reviewing and making suggestions
concerning the text of this book.

ISBN 0-695-40245-5 Titan binding
ISBN 0-695-80245-3 Trade binding

Library of Congress Catalog Card Number: 70-159323

First Printing

Contents

Introduction—
A Strange, Small World

HAVE YOU ever explored your backyard thoroughly? Did you look carefully to see the green cows, small lions, and flying bandits that live there? There are no cows or lions or bandits in your backyard? They are there, but many are smaller than the tip of your finger, for they are creatures of the insect world.

The world of insects is indeed a strange and odd one. Insects wear their skeletons on the outside of their bodies as sort of a rough, horny skin. They move their jaws sideways instead of up and down.

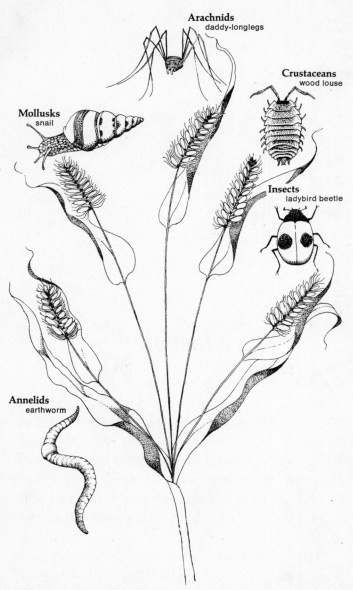

Arachnids
daddy-longlegs

Crustaceans
wood louse

Mollusks
snail

Insects
ladybird beetle

Annelids
earthworm

Animals belonging in these five invertebrate groups can be found in your backyard. Some annelids, mollusks, arachnids, and crustaceans are mistaken for insects.

Their blood is green, white, or yellow, but rarely red. They are the most numerous creatures of the animal world. Nine out of ten living creatures are insects. There may be as many as two million different kinds, and scientists haven't discovered all of them yet. They are heartily disliked by many humans who consider them to be pests. But only about 100 species of approximately 100,000 species in the United States do extensive damage.

Insects are included in the largest division of animals in the world, the phylum Arthropoda. This phylum, which contains segmented animals with jointed legs, is divided into classes, and insects are in the class called Insecta, or Hexapoda. This class in turn is divided into orders. There are about twenty-five orders of insects and about ten of these orders are of major importance.

Orders are divided into families, each family is divided into genera, and each genus is further divided into species. Most of the common insect names we use refer to either the family or the species. The specific Latin names may be helpful to a scientist, but it is a little difficult to say: order, Coleoptera; family, Scarabaeidae; genus, *Phyllophaga*; species, *fusca* when we are referring to one of the common May beetles! Sometimes, though, there are no common or English names for an insect.

All adult insects have three main body parts: a front section, or head; a middle section, or thorax;

and the hind section, or abdomen. Insects have no bones, but their bodies are covered with a material that looks like armor plate. The covering is the exoskeleton, and it is made of a substance called chitin. The exoskeleton is not in one piece, and the various parts can overlap each other to some extent. It is fairly rigid and will not stretch as the insect grows; therefore, the insect sheds, or molts, the covering when its body gets too big for it.

The head often contains the jaws, or mandibles, that move sideways, rather than up and down as in most other animals. But various insects have other types of mouth parts. For example, an adult mosquito has a beak that is used for drilling and sucking. A butterfly has a tubelike structure that is used as a siphon. A fly laps up its food.

Two antennae are connected to an insect's head. These are important sense organs, and various insects can smell, taste, feel, or hear with them. Other insects smell or taste with their feet, feel with the hairs on their bodies, or hear with organs on their legs or abdomens. It is not easy to find an insect's nose and ears!

Insects do not see as we do. Most mature insects have compound eyes that are made up of many eye facets, and each facet has its own lens. Each lens points in a slightly different direction. The separate images from each eye facet are put together in the brain to make a composite picture that looks like a mosaic, rather than looking like the single image that we would see. Insects, such as a fly or a bee, may have from 4,000 to as many as 13,000 facets in their eyes, and these facets may be different sizes. Although we do not know exactly how much or what they see, insects are particularly well equipped to see movement. This is necessary for their survival, because changing images in thousands of facets make them quickly aware of even slight movements.

Adult insects have three pairs of jointed legs attached to their thorax. How do these six-legged creatures move from place to place without getting their legs tangled? The legs work in a certain order. The first pair and the third pair usually move together, with the left leg of the first pair and the left leg of the third pair moving forward as the right leg of the first pair and the right leg of the third pair remain still and act as supports. The middle pair move just the opposite, with the left leg acting as a support while the right leg is moving forward. The way an insect uses his six legs to move about is quite different from the way we walk by balancing on one foot while moving the other forward. Insects with legs modified for digging, grasping, or swimming sometimes have difficulty walking.

Some insects have no wings, but most have two pairs. These wings come in different shapes and sizes. They can be transparent, hairy, scaly, or leathery. Veins in the wings are like slightly flexible struts

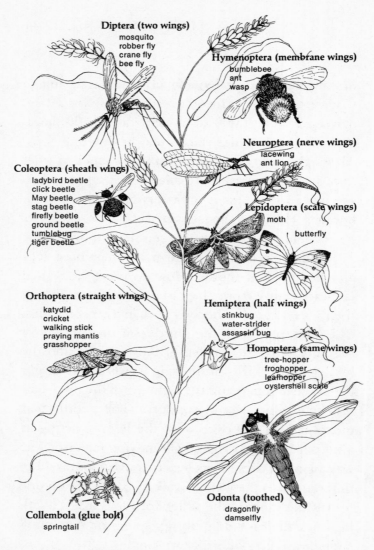

Diptera (two wings)
mosquito
robber fly
crane fly
bee fly

Hymenoptera (membrane wings)
bumblebee
ant
wasp

Neuroptera (nerve wings)
lacewing
ant lion

Coleoptera (sheath wings)
ladybird beetle
click beetle
May beetle
stag beetle
firefly beetle
ground beetle
tumblebug
tiger beetle

Lepidoptera (scale wings)
moth
butterfly

Orthoptera (straight wings)
katydid
cricket
walking stick
praying mantis
grasshopper

Hemiptera (half wings)
stinkbug
water-strider
assassin bug

Homoptera (same wings)
tree-hopper
froghopper
leafhopper
oystershell scale

Odonta (toothed)
dragonfly
damselfly

Collembola (glue bolt)
springtail

*This shows how various insects are related to each other
and how the major insect orders probably evolved. Those
at the top of the stem are more advanced than those
at the bottom.
In parentheses are the common names for the orders.*

and give the wings rigidity. The different vein patterns on the wings is one characteristic that scientists use to classify insects.

The wings are hinged to the thorax and move as the muscles attached to the top and bottom of the thorax contract. Wings do not beat straight up and down in an arc, either. If you have ever paddled a canoe, you know how to push back with the flat side of a paddle and then to turn the blade sideways as it comes forward so there is less air or water resistance against the blade's surface. This is similar to the way an insect's wings work.

If an insect has two pairs of wings, they overlap each other and work together. They cannot be used separately because too much air disturbance would make flight very difficult.

Some insects have only one pair of wings for flying. Through evolution their hind wings have been replaced by balancing organs known as halteres. The halteres vibrate in flight and act as very efficient gyroscopes when the insect changes direction.

The number and size of an insect's wings do not determine its capability for rapid flight. For example, the adult monarch butterfly has two pairs of wings, and it is a sturdy, strong flier that can cover great distances. It is capable of flying up to 650 miles without stopping. However, it only travels about six miles per hour on its long journeys. Many insects can fly faster than the monarch, particularly flies with only two wings.

Millions of years ago, when our planet was young, the only flying creatures were insects. Some of the earliest insects may have had three pairs of wings, one on each segment of the insect's thorax. Insects' wings developed specifically for flight. All other creatures that fly, such as birds and bats, have wings that are really modified legs.

An insect's internal organs are just as unique as its external body. The blood does not circulate throughout its body through veins, as a human's blood does. Instead, the blood is pumped by a tube that is its heart. After the blood has traveled through the tube to the head, it seeps out into the brain and other areas of the body. It then reenters the long tube again through small openings in the sides of the tube.

An insect breathes through a system of air tubes. It takes in air through openings along the sides of the body which are called spiracles. The air is carried directly to the tissues and organs in the body. It does not go through the blood and lungs as it does in our bodies. In some ways insects have a more efficient method of distributing oxygen where it is needed.

An insect's brain is small and has fewer cells than the brain of higher animals, but it is an intricate structure, nevertheless. Scientists are carefully studying the structure to learn more about insect's behavior. There are two enlarged nerve centers in the front portion of the body and a nerve cord running the length of the body. They make up the "central" nervous system. Insects are born with certain behavior patterns, or responses, that are built-in and do not have to be learned. They are programmed, much like a computer. But there is disagreement about whether or how much insects learn by experience or through reasoning. Some of their actions certainly appear to be very intelligent. However, careful study has shown that such behavior is mainly automatic, although even automatic, or instinctive behavior, is apparently modified at times.

An insect's digestive system is a long tube running from the mouth to the posterior of the insect. It has three main regions which vary according to the type of food the insect eats. Saliva is usually present to aid in breaking down the food, and many insects have a crop where food is stored before it is passed into a grinding organ, like a gizzard. When the food goes into the midgut, or second section, it is digested further and then passed on to the hindgut from which the wastes are eventually dispelled.

There are three ways an insect can develop and grow: direct development, incomplete metamorphosis, and complete metamorphosis. All insects begin as eggs, but they may develop in different ways.

A species can hatch and look like a miniature replica of its parent. It will not change its shape or appearance, but only grow larger. This is called direct development. But like all other insects, this kind does not grow gradually. It changes size in definite stages. The exoskeleton does not stretch as the insect grows; therefore, when the insect becomes too big for its rigid covering, it must break out, or molt. In direct development, an insect may molt many times in its life, and some continue to molt after reaching maturity and producing young.

Two names are frequently used for the young that hatch from eggs and develop by incomplete metamorphosis. Some are called nymphs, and they are all air breathers. The young grasshopper is called a nymph. Others, like the young dragonfly, are called naiads. The main difference is that naiads live in the water, breathe through gills, and do not look very much like their parents. Naiads live in a different environment than the one they will inhabit as adults.

If it is to be a winged insect, the wings begin to show as little buds during the nymph or naiad stage. The wings gradually develop until the last molt when they expand to their full size and are useful for flying. When the insect has fully-grown wings, it will not molt or grow any more. It has become an adult.

Complete metamorphosis is the most complicated type of development. Ants, bees, beetles, and butterflies are among the insects that develop by complete metamorphosis. The insect starts as an egg and hatches out as a larva. You would have a great deal of difficulty deciding what the parent looked like if you only saw the larva. There is no trace of wings, even if it will have wings as an adult. It chews, even if the adult sucks or eats some other way, or does not eat at all.

There are different names for different kinds of larvae. Some, such as butterflies, are called caterpillars, which means hairy cat. Some are called grubs, such as the larvae of the Mayfly or June bug. Some flies, in the larval stage, are known as maggots. The word *worm* is often used, too; but that is incorrect because it refers to other creatures, not insects.

As they grow, larvae molt and develop into the pupal stage. The word *pupa* is Latin and means baby or child. The famous scientist Linnaeus used this term because the insect at this stage reminded him of a baby or papoose wrapped up.

The pupal stage is usually a resting or inactive period. But the pupae of some insects do remain active, such as mosquitoes, and some others may crawl about a bit before the last big transformation takes place. The insect does not feed at this time and it is usually quite delicate and helpless. It may have a shrunken or dried-up appearance. Even though it is considered a resting time, very great changes are going on inside. Extra legs, such as the prolegs of the caterpillar, are lost, and some others will acquire legs they did not have before. A different kind of mouth part may develop, and some will now acquire wings for the first time. Old parts break down and new ones form. There is a final molt at the end of the pupal stage, and when the insect emerges it is mature.

Insects grow by definite steps or stages, rather than by the gradual development that takes place in most warm-blooded creatures. They can also stop developing. This is known as diapause, a dormant state that can occur at any stage of the insect's life. It may happen because of adverse weather conditions, diet deficiency, too much or too little daylight. It prevents the insect from developing further if conditions are not favorable. Then when the environment is better, it will start growing again, taking up where it left off, whether it has been dormant a few weeks or several seasons.

What an insect does is often determined by the weather. You have probably already noticed how much more activity there seems to be on a warm day; the caterpillars eat faster, ants run faster, and crickets chirp faster. The body temperatures of most insects are about equal to that of their surroundings, but some can warm themselves up somewhat by moving their muscles or wings. Others, such as bumblebees, have a furry coat that helps

Complete Metamorphosis

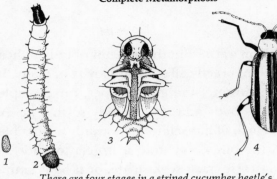

There are four stages in a striped cucumber beetle's development: egg (1), larva (2), pupa (3), and adult (4).

Incomplete Metamorphosis

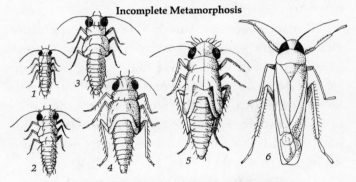

There are three stages in a leafhopper's development: egg (not shown), nymph (1-5), and adult (6).

Direct Development

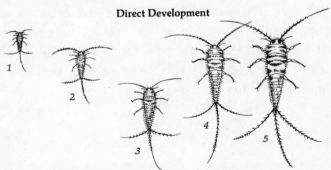

A newly hatched silverfish (1) looks like an adult silverfish (5), except it is much smaller. After leaving its egg (not shown), the silverfish will molt several times (2-4) before reaching maturity.

to keep them warm. But the amount of radiant heat from the sun directly affects the activity of many. In the early morning, the grasshopper, for example, will turn his body and lean slightly so that he exposes as much of himself to the warmth as possible. It works the other way, too; if it gets too hot, he might roast. He must seek shade, or if he is sitting on very hot sand, he will jump into the air every so often to cool off.

If insects are so susceptible to temperature changes, how can they survive a freezing winter? Most of them cannot. Those that survive over winter can do so only by hibernating, usually in egg or larval form. In their hibernating stage, some produce a substance similar to the antifreeze that is put into the radiator of a car to keep it from freezing up in severe weather.

The life span of insects varies greatly. Some have very short lives; others, such as the cicada, live for over ten years. We tend to think of adult as meaning the grown-up period and the longest part of a life. But this is not true for insects. The adult insect may live for a very brief period, perhaps a matter of hours or days.

1

Battle on the Rosebush

LOOKING for insects can be a real adventure. And if you look at them very closely you will make some interesting discoveries. By searching up and down and all around—on plants or flowers, in the ground or in the air, under logs or bark or stones—you might find a hundred different kinds of insects in one afternoon. That may seem like a lot, but an entomologist, a person who studies insects, might find many more in the same area. There may be more insects in your backyard than there are people in your hometown!

A magnifying glass is the only equipment you will really need for your backyard exploring. Perhaps you might want a large wide-mouthed glass bottle, too. Sometimes the insects do not stay in one place long enough for you to see them clearly. You can capture these and put them in the bottle. After watching them closely you can free them. A rosebush in the backyard is a good starting place for your adventures.

GREEN COWS
(Aphids)

You may find some tiny, pale green insects bunched together on the buds, leaves, or soft stems of the rosebush. These are aphids, or plant lice. Some may be so small that they are mere specks; others may be fully grown and easier to see. Look very closely at the adults and you will be able to see their legs and antennae, or feelers, which look like tiny threads.

The mouths of aphids are like beaks, and they are used to suck the sap, or juices from the plant, just as you might sip lemonade through a straw. It takes a great amount of sap to feed an aphid because sap is mostly water. They have a built-in filter to separate the water from the protein in the sap sugar. As they feed, the water and some of the excess sap carbohydrate are secreted from their bodies in the form of droplets known as honeydew.

Aphids do not move around much. They spend most of their time seeking nourishment and propagating. They are capable of multiplying very rapidly. In the spring they hatch out from eggs laid the year before, but during the summer some female aphids produce live young. This is very unusual, and scientists cannot yet explain why it is possible for some aphids to be hatched from eggs and others to be born alive.

A few days after a young female aphid is born she produces aphids. Soon a whole army of aphids may cover a rosebush. An aphid army is in a constant state of siege. Gardeners consider them pests because they may cause wilting of plants or spread

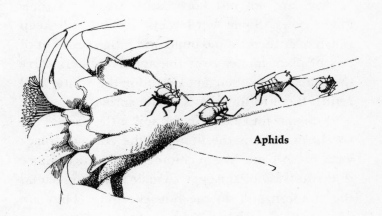

Aphids

plant diseases; so they spray them with insecticides. Many birds and some insects prey upon aphids and eat them.

Aphids have one friend, however. Somewhere on or near the rosebush there will be ants.

INSECT FARMERS

(Yard Ants)

Some yard ants are very fond of the honeydew that aphids secrete. They will stroke the back of an aphid with their antennae, to get a drop of honeydew, much as a farmer milks a cow. A good aphid "cow" has been known to give forty-eight drops of honeydew in twenty-four hours. You may have to observe a long time to see this happen, but the yard ants will be milking the aphids at various times throughout the summer in your yard.

Ants are not just fair-weather friends of their green cows. Some herd their "cows" and keep watch over them; some build odd little sheds out of bits of plant matter over the aphids. Others carry the aphids into their ant nests for the winter and return them to the plants in the spring.

You may find a nest in the soil at the base of the rosebush. This is the home of the common black yard ant. All ants live in colonies, with one or more queen ants laying the eggs. Female worker ants tend the children and do the housekeeping. They are running up and down the rosebush stem collecting honeydew to feed the larvae, which are the immature, wingless ants that hatch from the eggs. The male ants do not do any work, and so they do not live long after they mate with the females.

When a large number of ants with wings leave an old nest, it is called swarming. Mating usually takes place during this flight. The young female queen ant then kicks off her wings, digs out a small cell in the ground by herself, and lays a few eggs. When the eggs hatch into larvae she feeds them

Yard Ant and Aphid

digested food from her mouth. The first larvae become worker ants when they are fully grown. Then the queen ant has a colony and is not bothered with the details of making a living since she is cared for by her children. All she has to do is lay more eggs, and the worker ants supply the food for the colony.

Look under an old board or piece of rotten wood and you may discover a nest of carpenter ants. When this nest is disturbed, the worker ants will gather up the eggs and the larvae and quickly take them to a safe place. You may be able to see the hooked bristles on the larvae which the worker ants use as handles when they haul their helpless charges around.

Ants do not see very well; some, in fact, are blind. Their antennae, which contain their smelling organs, are more useful to them than their eyes when they move around on top of and in the ground. Ants "tap talk" to each other with their feelers.

A war between black ants and red ants will be worth watching if you come upon one sometime. The red ants are usually the winners. After they have killed or scattered all the black ants, they raid the nests and carry away the young of the black ants. They raise the black ants in their own homes to be their servants and slaves.

SOLDIERS IN ORANGE ARMOR

(Ladybird Beetles)

If you have found a cluster of aphids on the rosebush, you will not have to look far to find a ladybird beetle. Ladybird beetles are dangerous enemies of the aphids. One ladybird can destroy as many as 100 aphids in a day.

Hundreds of years ago the people of Europe dedicated the ladybird beetle to the Virgin Mary because the ladybirds were so helpful in destroying the pesty aphids found on the crops. They were known as Beetles of Our Lady, and that is why they are called ladybirds or ladybugs today.

In some parts of the United States ladybird beetles are collected and sold by the pound. Then they are purchased by gardeners who put them on plants and trees to fight destructive insects. Ladybirds are not hard to gather, for in the fall they hibernate in big groups in high places. Sometimes you can find them in the summer in your backyard under low bushes or old wood.

Each variety of ladybird beetle wears a different polka-dot combination; the ones you find may have two spots, nine spots, fifteen spots, or "hit-and-miss" spots. Ladybirds are useful insects, but unfortunately they have some look-alike relatives that are leaf-eaters. The Mexican bean beetle, with sixteen spots, and the squash ladybird, with twelve spots, are the "black sheep" of the family. They can be found lunching on the underside of the foliage of garden peas and squash.

Some insects are friends and others are considered pests. The pests are those that do something that bothers us, such as eating plants we grow or carrying disease. Though we hear more about the pests in the insect world, only a relatively few are destructive or harmful. Some of these can do a great deal of damage, however.

Still, it's largely a matter of viewpoint. If an insect feeds on grain grown in a field, it is a pest; but, if it eats only weeds along the edge of the field or eats the insects that eat the wheat, it is a friend. Certainly the ladybird beetle is a pest to the aphid, but it is a good friend to man. Some of the poisonous sprays that farmers and gardeners use kill both the friends and foes of man.

Near the ladybird beetle you will find some of her larval children. They resemble miniature scaly alligators. The ladybird lays her yellow eggs near a cluster of aphids so there will be plenty of food for her children when they hatch. And they go right to work on the aphids, too.

Remember the old nursery rhyme:

"Ladybird, ladybird, fly away home,
Your house is on fire, your children will burn."

This rhyme started in Europe where they burn the hop vines after the harvest. The vines are usually full of aphids, and also ladybird beetle children. The burning vine is the "house on fire." The larval babies on the vines have no wings and cannot fly away; so the ladybird beetle "children will burn."

The bright colors of a ladybird beetle are a form of advertisement. Ladybird beetles do not taste good; so the black and orange is warning for birds and other creatures which might be tempted to eat them. Of course, there is no accounting for tastes. After all, people learn to like such strange things as green olives or Limburger cheese. If some creature acquires a taste for ladybird beetles, then her bright colors will be an invitation to dinner instead of a warning.

Nudge a ladybird beetle a little and she will fly off a short distance. When she lands it may look as if her slip is showing. A ladybird, like many insects, has two pairs of wings. The bright hard ones are on the outside, and they must be raised and held up

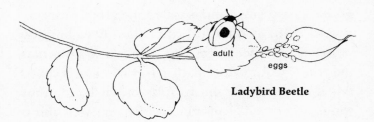

adult

eggs

Ladybird Beetle

and out of the way when she wants to fly. The second pair of wings is used for flying. It is soft, thin, and larger than the other pair. When the insect is not flying, the larger wings are folded underneath the other pair. In this beetle's constant hurry and scurry, she does not always take time to tuck her wings in properly.

THE LION WITH NO ROAR

(Green Lacewing Fly)

Small, brown creatures covered with short, bristly hairs may be found stalking among the aphids on the rosebush, too. If you watch them very closely you will soon see why they are called aphis-lions. The name suits them very well. They pounce on the aphids with curved fangs, drain them of their blood, and toss their exoskeletons away. Aphis-lions are so bloodthirsty that they will even eat each other.

The mother of these ferocious children is easily found at night near a lighted window, but perhaps one or two will be found in the bushes during the day. She is a delicate little insect with two pairs of green, gauzy wings and is called the green lacewing fly. Also, she is often called Golden Eyes because of her large golden-red eyes. She is also known as the stink fly. And you can discover why she is called this if you pick one up. In spite of her large, filmy wings, the green lacewing can't fly very well and is pushed around by wind currents. She can only fly about one mile an hour on her own in calm air, which is very slow in comparison to most flying insects.

Look now for the eggs that a lacewing fly has laid, for they will be somewhere nearby. They will look like tiny white plants with stems. For many years scientists believed that they were some kind of plant. One day someone was watching a green lacewing fly very carefully and discovered that she laid her eggs in a strange way. She expels a sticky substance; draws it up into a thin threadlike stalk about one-half inch long which hardens when exposed to the air. Then she lays an egg on the very tip of the thread. Raising the stalks up in the air helps to protect the eggs from other insects or even from her own children.

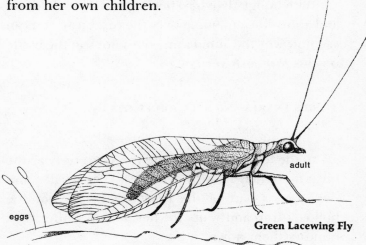

eggs

adult

Green Lacewing Fly

Break off a leaf stalk that the eggs are fastened
upon and put it in a glass jar. In a few days you will
see an egg hatch, and the larva crawl down the stem.
If you want to watch aphis-lions grow you will have
to keep them well supplied with food. A newly
hatched larva will start by eating two or three aphids
a day. In ten or twelve days it is able to eat as many
as 100. By that time it is well fed. It then spins itself
into a silky cocoon and in about fifteen days a pretty
adult lacewing will emerge.

There doesn't seem to be much relation between the ferocious young aphis-lion and the pretty
green adult. But in the insect world many insect
children are very different in form from their parents. It is unlikely that even a lacewing fly mother
would know her own offspring.

With hungry ladybird beetles and their children,
and aphis-lions roaming over the rosebush, you can
see now why the aphid army does not win the battle
on the rosebush very often.

SILK SNARES AND BALLOON PILOTS
(Garden Spider)

In the low branches of the rosebush or near the
bush there may be a spider's nest. The garden spider, too, is part of the rosebush battle, but she
builds a trap and waits for her victims rather than
hunting them down.

The spider is different in many ways from the insects we have found so far. In fact, she is not an insect. How can you tell? The easiest way is to count the number of legs. The lacewing fly, the ladybird, the ant, and the aphid all have three pairs of legs, but all spiders have four pairs. Most insects have wings, but spiders do not. There is also another difference that is important to scientists who sort out and classify all the creatures in the world. Spiders have only two main body divisions. Adult insects have three main divisions. This may not be easy to see, and sometimes has to be proven by careful examination under a microscope.

Insects and spiders are both members of the animal kingdom. Insects belong to a class called Insecta. Most people call just about any insect a bug. But bugs are only one kind of insect, and there are not as many different kinds of true bugs as you may think. This is not as important to us as it is to the people who are trying to arrange insects neatly in lists and tables. These people have a big job because new insects keep being discovered that just don't seem to fit properly.

Spiders have close relatives, such as ticks, chiggers, scorpions, and daddy-longlegs. They all belong to a class called Arachnida. This name comes from an old Greek myth about a girl named Arachne. She was very proud of her ability to spin and weave. One day she challenged the goddess

Athena to a weaving contest. This proved to be quite unwise, for the goddess tore up Arachne's beautiful woven piece in a fit of jealous rage. Arachne then hung herself in despair and disgrace. The goddess took pity on her, however, loosened the rope around Arachne's neck and changed the girl into a spider.

The garden spider always spins her web at the same time of day, although the time will depend on which kind of garden spider she is. One spider in the yard may take up its post underneath a light. Night after night she will spin a web as soon as it is dark. When she has completed the web, she will wait for a victim to get caught in it. After this happens she will scramble all over the web and tie up the victim. By morning the web will be gone, except for three or four long framework strands marking the area where she will be working again after dark. The spider will remain quiet during the day in a corner under the house eaves or some other shady area.

When the spider spins her web, she starts by making a frame in the shape of a triangle or square. Then she lays out spokes in all directions. The spider drops free on a silk dragline only once. This is where she lays the first cross spoke that divides the framework. Then she climbs along the lines she has already made. Dragging the next spoke behind herself, the spider reels it in and fastens it in the proper place.

Starting at the center of the frame she weaves a rough spiral that connects all the spokes going out from the center. But this is not part of the permanent web; it is only the temporary scaffolding to hold the spokes in place. The real snare is made when the spider starts spinning from the outside and makes the spiral toward the center. These lines are sticky because she puts droplets of an adhesive substance on them. This substance causes real trouble for a fly that comes into the web. As the spider works in toward the center, she rolls up the scaffolding threads. She doesn't stick to the gluey threads of her web because a spider's feet are coated with an oily substance that keeps her from becoming entangled. She is careful, too, to keep her feet planted on the dry lines or spokes of her web. The spider does not bother to repair any holes in her web, either. She simply remakes the whole thing later.

Some garden spiders make a little silk pad in the center of the web on which they sit. Others spin a "telephone line" from the web to a hiding place. A garden spider has very poor eyesight and depends on the vibrations of the web threads to tell her when something is caught. When she gets the signal, she rushes out to examine the struggling insect. If it is a wasp or a bee, she may want no part of it and either cuts the visitor loose or lets it struggle out as best it can. Most other insects are fair game for the spider.

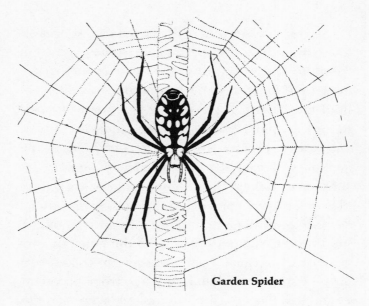

Garden Spider

She throws wide bands of silk around the victim until it is trussed up like a mummy. Then she has a feast. If she has eaten recently and isn't hungry, she may hang it up in the web for a future meal. Spiders do not suck the blood of their prey. They predigest it by injecting a fluid into the body of the insect. This fluid dissolves the tissues, and then the body is pumped dry, leaving only a hollow shell.

Various spiders can spin many kinds of silk. There is elastic silk, sticky silk, thick silk, downy cocoon silk, colored silk, and soft silk. Spider silk is stronger and finer than that made by silkworms; it has a greater tensile strength then steel. Spider silk is often used as cross hairs in telescopic gunsights.

There are more than 2,500 kinds of spiders. We usually think of webs when we think of spiders, but most spiders do not spin webs. Some hunt down their victims, as the wolf spiders and jumping spiders do; others, like the crab spider, hide and wait for their prey.

Late in the summer the female garden spider lays her eggs inside a silk egg sac. The spider guards the eggs until she dies in the fall. But some spiders carry the egg sac around on their backs.

Some baby spiders, or spiderlings, become "balloon pilots" soon after they hatch. Have you ever seen the air filled with tiny cobweb threads? They stream from bushes and brush across your face as you walk between trees. These are threads that tiny spiderlings spin to serve as balloons.

Hundreds of little spiderlings may hatch at the same time in the same area. There would not be enough food if they all remained in one place. One day when the sun is warm and the air currents are moving upward, the spiderlings climb to the tip of a tall bush or a high stalk of grass, face the breeze, and spin out a fine thread. The wind catches the thread, the spiderlings let go of their perches and sail off on their silk balloons.

The spiderling is at the mercy of the air currents, but he can control his sail by pulling in thread or letting out more. Sometimes the spiderlings go only a few yards, but others may go sailing for hundreds of miles. They have been found far out at sea.

A spider's bite is highly overrated. Most are not harmful, few are even painful, and only one or two rather shy ones in North America are dangerous. The nursery rhyme about Miss Muffet who sat on her tuffet is not fair to either the spider or Miss Muffet. She was the daughter of a Reverend Mouffet who lived in the sixteenth century. He studied and described spiders and their activities. Thus, it is hard to believe that the daughter of a man who admired and understood spiders could be frightened away by the spider who sat down beside her.

MUD PIES AND HYPODERMIC NEEDLES
(Mud-Dauber Wasp)

The garden spider may find the rosebush a good hunting ground, but a certain visitor to the bush can turn the tables and the hunter will become the hunted. The mud-dauber wasp is the hunter who searches for garden spiders, in order to stock the larder of her nursery.

The mud-dauber may be found flying around the rosebush, or she may be busy in a nearby mud puddle. The best way to watch her at work is to find her house. Look under the eaves or on the walls of an old shed until you find a mud house.

The mud-dauber is a solitary wasp; that is, she lives by herself and works alone. In fact, most wasps are solitary. But we are most apt to know, and avoid, the "social" wasps. These are the hornets, the yellow jackets and the paper wasps, some of which build large houses and live together in colonies.

The mud-dauber collects a small ball of mud which she carries back to the place she has selected for her nursery. Slowly she pats and shapes it, sometimes buzzing as she works. She builds a flat foundation. Then she makes a ring of mud, and then another, until she has built up a hollow mud cell. This is the first room of her nursery. She does not start another until this is completely finished and furnished. Now she will stock it with food, lay her egg, and seal it up.

The mud-dauber has a very ingenious way of providing fresh food for her babies. She swoops down on a spider, seizes it, and plunges her stinger twice into the spider's body. She injects only enough poison in just the right places to paralyze, but not kill the spider. A doctor uses a hypodermic needle to deaden certain nerves in our bodies in much the same way. The wasp places the helpless spider in the mud cell she has made. The spider is still alive and will be alive as long as it is needed,

Mud-Dauber Wasp

but it is not able to move. The wasp then lays her egg. When the tiny wasp larva hatches, about three days later, it has a fresh spider meal waiting. Strangely enough, mother wasp dines only on nectar, but her babies are meat eaters.

Now the wasp goes on to construct another cell in her nursery. Meanwhile, in the first, the larva that has hatched from the egg feeds for a week or two. It grows about six times bigger than its size at hatching and then encases itself in a silk cocoon. It lives there quietly in the dark throughout the winter. Then on a spring morning it wriggles about and splits its cocoon. Now its appearance is similar to an adult wasp, except that it is colorless. During the next four weeks its body will grow and turn yellow and black in the appropriate areas. Finally, it cuts out of its cell, lets its wings dry and harden in the air, and flies off.

Take down a nest and examine it under your magnifying glass, but do be sure that you have the right kind of wasp nest! You will be able to count the mud rings in each cell. In early summer you may find a wasp egg and the spider that will be its food. Or you may uncover the larva; it will be a tiny, whitish, wormlike creature without legs. Later in the summer inside the cocoon it has spun the larva will look like a pale sac filled with fluid. And there will be no sign of the spider. On a May day of the following year you might open a cell to find the pupa, an almost transparent wasp with four thick pads where its wings will be. In June you will find a restless little creature ready to come out; this will be the adult wasp.

THE FLYING BANDIT

(Robber Fly)

On the tip of a branch of the rosebush, the sharp-eyed robber fly may be poised, watching for a victim. Perhaps the mud-dauber wasp will now be the hunted instead of the hunter. The robber fly is a fast, fearless bandit of the air.

It is well built for hunting on the wing. It can fly very fast and has long powerful legs with which to clasp its prey in midair. Fortunately for us, this ferocious hunter is only interested in other insects.

When a robber fly spies a possible meal, it swoops swiftly and usually makes a capture on the first try. It stabs the victim with its beak, then returns to its perch to enjoy dinner. It has a big appetite, and sometimes a small pile of exoskeletons may be found underneath its favorite lookout perch. Occasionally this fly will steal a victim from another insect. That is why it is called a robber fly.

It is not easy to watch this fly in action, for it moves as if it were jet-propelled. Your best chance to watch him will be after he has captured an insect and is busy eating it. Or you may find him early on

Robber Fly

a cool morning inside the rose blossom where he has lodged for the night.

If you have searched around the rosebush carefully, you have already found many other insects. We will look at some of them closely. You will want to look up others in the guide books that list many more kinds of insects. There is no such thing as an ordinary insect, even the ones we see most often have extraordinary habits.

Insect behavior varies. Some of the mysteries have been solved just by careful observance, but there are just as many mysteries yet to be solved. Your backyard is full of adventures, and it may also hold the answer to some insect riddles, if you look closely.

2

Sound All Around

YOU CAN explore your backyard by following your ears as well as your eyes. In fact, it will help if you shut your eyes and just listen for a while. On a quiet day the air will be full of hums, chirps, whines, and buzzings.

Insects make different noises for different reasons and in very different ways. They have no vocal chords, as humans do. They vibrate built-in drums or use their wings or legs. Some insect noises are made for courting purposes or as a defense against enemies.

CHEERFUL CHIRPS

(Black Field Cricket)

The "chirp, chirp" of the black field cricket will probably be the first sound you hear when you stop to listen to the chorus in your yard. The cricket tunes up about mid-July, and it may even sing outdoors during early winter from some sheltered nook.

A cricket sings with his wings. And he does it in much the same way that you can make a high-pitched noise by running a sharp object over a metal file. The cricket has two pairs of wings, and the front, or upper wings, are the sound makers. There are little ridges, like the ridges of a file, on the underside of each wing. There is also another thickened area, like a scraper, on the edge of the wings. The cricket moves his wings rapidly from side to

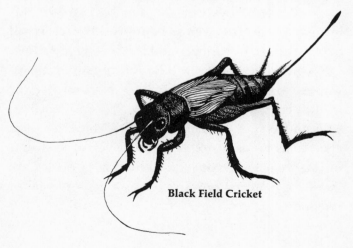

Black Field Cricket

side, rubbing them across each other so that they vibrate and make a rasping noise. The pitch is raised and lowered by the speed with which he vibrates his wings. He can sound very close or very far away, like ventriloquists who "throw" their voices. Often he sings while sitting in crevices or hollows which amplify his song.

Female crickets don't sing, but they listen with an organ near their knees! Most species have eardrums in their front legs. The wings of the female are shorter than the "singing" wings of the male. You can also tell her from the male by the long slender tube that extends from her body. This is called an ovipositor. That rhymes with egg depositor, which is just what it is. The female cricket uses it to poke holes in the ground and to lay her eggs.

The young crickets are able to take care of themselves as soon as they are hatched. They wander around all summer gradually growing larger and shedding their outside skeletons several times. After the last molt, the young males begin to tune up. They may sound a bit scratchy at first, but after a few days' practice they are accomplished musicians and their sound attracts the female crickets.

Temperature has a great deal to do with the way a cricket behaves, just as it does with all insects. The cricket can even serve as a makeshift thermometer. A close relative of the black field cricket is called the temperature cricket because he is considered a rather accurate thermometer. He works the night shift late in the summer and is usually found in trees and low bushes. He often sings in a chorus, and if the sound seems to be coming from all around, it is! Snowy tree crickets, as they are also called, often chirp together with a shrill, monotonous, and persistent "chee, chee, chee." If you can tell the chirps apart and have a watch with a second hand available, count the number of chirps in fifteen seconds, and add forty. The number you get will equal the air temperature. This is a good trick to display to your friends some warm evening. If you listen for crickets and watch the temperature, you'll soon discover that crickets don't chirp when it is colder than 55° F. or when it is warmer than 100° F.

The snowy tree cricket is shy and rather difficult to find. It is a pale transparent green that blends well with the surroundings, where it is easily heard but seldom seen!

Why do crickets sing? Scientists say they have one song to attract mates and another to warn off rivals. They also seem to enjoy the sound of their own voices. They are curious, too, and explore everything with their feelers. If you watch a cricket come up to another insect, it looks like he deliberately tickles the other fellow.

Crickets don't usually fly; they run or jump. They live alone or perhaps as a pair the first part of the summer in little burrows that they dig in the ground. Later they are more sociable and may gather together in larger groups.

They are not particularly fussy about their food, and they eat plant foliage, small seeds of grain, small insects, and sometimes cloth when they get into the house.

Watch a cricket clean himself. He is very particular about his appearance, and goes through acrobatic motions to get at the various parts of his body. Male crickets sometimes can be seen fighting, but their battles are more bluster than fight. They seldom damage each other, and the best bluffer forces the other to retreat to his burrow. In China they have cricket fights similar to the cock rooster fights in other parts of the world. These crickets, like the roosters, are especially bred to be fierce.

Mole crickets, sand crickets, and cave crickets are some of the other kinds you may find. The black field cricket makes a lively and interesting pet, and people from all over the world have kept them in cages to watch their antics and listen to their cheerful chirps.

MORE FIDDLERS

(Angular-Winged Katydid)

You just can't help hearing a close relative of the cricket after dusk from the middle of the summer on. This is the katydid, which is a long-horned grasshopper. He does resemble a common short-horned grasshopper, but you can tell them apart by the greater length of the katydid's antennae, which are as long or longer than his body. He is usually green and cannot jump nearly as well as a short horned grasshopper.

Each kind of katydid makes its own distinctive sound and cannot start to sing until it is fully developed. The one most likely to be in the low bushes near your house or even on a window screen is the angular-winged katydid who says "tic-tzeet." He starts slowly with a few "tics" and then goes faster and faster with long "tzeets" and then suddenly stops. Like the cricket, the katydid fiddles his song with his wings and listens with his knees. Katydids

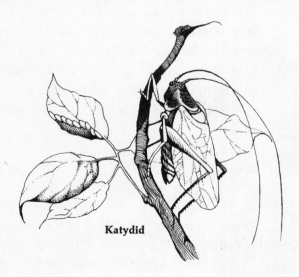

Katydid

have a miniature amplifier in the base of their wings. It's a disc-shaped device that acts like a tiny megaphone. Without this the katydid's song would be a scratching noise you couldn't even hear. Instead it becomes a crackling "tzeet" that might be heard almost a mile away.

The female katydid lays flat, oval-shaped eggs, which almost look like tree buds, in neat overlapping rows along a twig or the edge of a leaf. The young katydid hatches in the spring. During the summer it feeds and grows and sheds its skin. The wing cases bulge and the wings develop. The angular-winged katydid folds these over its back like a tent. You will never find a cast-off katydid skin. Katydids eat them, leaving no traces of their former selves.

One of the most interesting things you can watch in your backyard is an insect in the process of molting. Perhaps you may see a katydid doing this; if not, try to capture one early in the summer before it has its wings. Put it in a cage, feed it, and note its activities.

When a katydid is ready to molt, the skin splits down the back of the thorax and where the head and thorax meet. The head slides out of the old covering first. Then the katydid carefully withdraws its long antennae. The katydid jerks and wiggles, holding on to its support with two pairs of back legs. It moves the body forward out of the old skin a bit.

Now the front pair of legs are pulled out and the worst is over. Holding on to a twig with its front legs, it can pull and twist the rest of its body and other legs free. A few minutes to rest, to suck in air and expand its new wrinkled skin, to let the skeleton harden and the wings expand, and then it is off about its business again.

AN INSECT RIP VAN WINKLE

(Cicada)

The steady, monotonous drone that you hear on a warm day is made by an insect with a drum, the cicada. He has round membranes stretched over two openings in his body at the base of his abdomen. He vibrates these in and out with a set of strong muscles. If you bend the bottom of a tin pie plate back and forth, you will see how he makes his noise. He often starts softly, like a distant buzz saw, and works up to an earsplitting climax.

Only the male drums. He can control the volume of his drumming and seems to throw the sound around so it is often hard to tell where he is. Cicadas may not actually hear the noise they make as we hear it, but only receive sound vibrations.

The cicada is a sap-sucking bug. But his common names are very confusing, for he is also called a harvest fly and a locust. Short-horned grasshoppers are usually called locusts; the plague of locusts mentioned in the Bible was a plague of grasshoppers. However some say our forefathers mistook a horde of 17-year-cicadas for a plague of locusts. So we still hear talk about the "17-year-locust" which isn't a locust at all but a cicada.

The cicada is an insect Rip Van Winkle. The female makes a slit in the young twigs of a tree with her chisel-like ovipositor and lays her eggs in this crack. This action causes much destruction for nurserymen, because the slits weaken the small branches and they tend to break off in a high wind.

The eggs hatch and the nymphs, as the young of this kind of insect are called, drop to the ground. There they burrow in to find a suitable root from which to suck sap. And they stay there from two to twenty years, depending on the species! No other

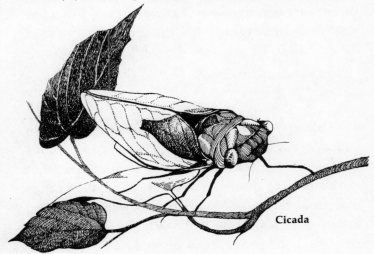

Cicada

insect takes so long to grow up. As many as seven molts may take place underground. When they reappear, it is quite a "coming out" party. Thousands may emerge from the ground under a large tree. The sight of such a swarm is not apt to be forgotten. Now they crawl up a tree trunk or other support and make a final molt, emerging with wings. Their old empty coverings look like "cellophane ghosts" attached to shrubs and trees in the area.

If the cicada you find has red eyes and reddish-yellow veins on the wings, it is a periodical cicada and has been out of sight for thirteen to twenty years. But if it is greenish and lacks the bright color, it is one of the annual cicadas or harvest flies. Even with the name annual cicada it has spent two or three years underground. The adult lives only a few weeks after emerging from the ground.

BEEBREAD AND BASKETS

(Bumblebee)

The air is full of humming noises on a warm summer day. The biggest and most conspicuous hummer is the bumblebee. The hum comes from the air passing through the bee's two pairs of wings and from air forced out of the breathing pores, called spiracles, along its body.

A bumblebee seems to be well named. It bumbles around a bit aimlessly and rather awkwardly most of the time. It looks comical standing on its head inside a flower blossom. It is even surprising that a bumblebee can fly at all, for it is bulky in the body and its wings are small.

Man has discovered many facts about the laws of flight. But he had to study the angle of wings during flight and their rate of vibration to prove to himself that a bumblebee could fly. Of course, the bumblebee knew it all the time. Insects have known about flying a lot longer than man!

Bumblebees are social insects; they live together in colonies in the soil. Many kinds of bees are solitary, just as the mud-dauber wasp is a solitary wasp. The honeybees have a much more complicated and elaborate way of living together than the bumblebees, but they do have many things in common.

The very large bumblebees that you see in the spring and early summer are queen bees that have come out of hibernation. After eight or nine months underground, they are hungry and ready to start a new bumblebee colony. The young queen searches for a suitable nesting place in the ground, such as an abandoned mouse hole. When she finds a burrow that will do, she fixes a comfortable bed of moss and grass for herself. Then she builds a waxen honeypot, gathers her raw materials and fills the honeypot. She also prepares some beebread. She kneads pollen with nectar into a paste, lays her eggs on the surface of the paste, spreads a wax covering over the eggs, and proceeds to sit on them like a mother hen.

She sits four or five days, sipping at the honey which she has stored in the waxen pot close by. When the eggs hatch, the larvae eat the beebread she has prepared. The queen still keeps the larvae sealed in little wax cells, but now she must add to her babies' diet. She makes more beebread and gives them honey. She must bite a hole in the wax and seal it up each time she feeds them. In about eleven days the larvae spin cocoons. The queen bee continues to sit on them.

The first brood that emerges are all workers, and they are small females. With each new brood there are more workers to help with the food supply. The bees that are born in the middle or late summer develop into queens and drones, or male bees.

A bumblebee colony may have from 100 to 500 bees, and it is a one-season colony. The new young queens and the male drones leave the nest in late summer. Mating takes place during flight, the drones die, and each queen goes into an underground burrow. The old colony dies out gradually, and scavengers, such as beetles, destroy the nest.

A bumblebee queen is not treated as royally as ant queens or honeybee queens. She has to help gather pollen and nectar. She even has to comb and groom herself.

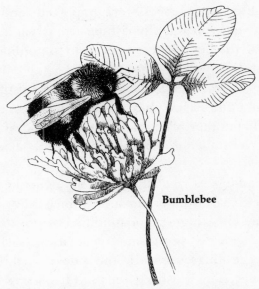

Bumblebee

Bumblebees gather both pollen and nectar from the blossoms they visit. The pollen sticks to their furry bodies, and they comb it out and stuff it into little pollen baskets that are attached to their hind legs. They don't get all the pollen off their bodies, and some of it is smeared onto the next blossoms they visit. In this way bees pollinate many plants.

Bumblebees have exceptionally long tongues which are like tubes. They suck up the nectar with these. They are the only bees which can easily reach the nectar in red clover, and they are very fond of it. Without the assistance of the bumblebees there would be very few red clover seeds. Farmers in New Zealand once had a great deal of trouble growing red clover, even though the conditions were very favorable. Bumblebees were imported, and soon the clover crop was flourishing from year to year because the bumblebees were able to pollinate the plants.

Bees have a tendency to visit one kind of blossom at a time. Thus they spread the pollen of that plant to another of the same kind, instead of carrying clover pollen to a bean blossom or a daisy blossom.

Bumblebees, like all insects, have enemies. The females have a stinger, however, which is good protection. The stinger is the modified ovipositor. It is a shaft with two prongs and grooves on each one. When she stings, she works one side down and then the other. The poison is released from sacs at the base of the stinger, and runs down the grooves in each side. Her stinger is about one-fourth inch long and sharper than a needle. A bumblebee sting is temporarily painful but not usually dangerous.

A bumblebee is good natured and intent upon her business. Furthermore, her hum is a clue to the state of her temper. There is little reason to be stung while watching her, but if you are doubtful, you can get close while she is busy inside a blossom. You will find a dead bumblebee from time to time, which is safe to handle. With a magnifying glass you can examine the stinger, long tongue, pollen basket, and the combs on its legs.

How do bees make a "bee line" back to their nests after wandering all over a field? Can they see different colors? Do they tell time? These are some of the questions that are still partly mysteries. Experiments seem to show that bees, loaded with pollen and nectar, find the way home by remembering certain landmarks. Also, the direction of light rays, although not necessarily direct light from the sun, helps them find their way. Bees can see colors, but apparently they do not see colors in the same way that we do. Bees and many insects can see ultraviolet which does not register on our eyes at all. They also seem to recognize certain flowers by the number and arrangement of the petals. They are able to tell each other where and how far to go to find the best flowers. Honeybees communicate by a dance pattern combining loops and circles and tail wagging. Some experiments indicate that bees may have a form of built-in clock or time memory that guides their activities during the day.

Some backyard insect mysteries have been solved in the past, but others provide as much adventure right now for scientists as they may for you.

THE NOISE THAT ANNOYS

(Mosquito)

An insect with a most annoying noise is the mosquito. This time it is the female that is solely responsible for the whining, buzzing, and the unpleasant bite.

Some sounds of insects are not intentional, but

the female mosquito "sings" on purpose. She has two kinds of songs. One is a love-call to a male mosquito and the other is a blood-call to other females announcing that she has found meat, which means blood.

Each kind of mosquito sings its own song. The males have antennae which pick up the sound waves of their own kind. Mosquito songs have been used to trap them. Tape recordings of the songs have been made, and when they are played back, both the male and the female mosquitoes come a-flying.

Only the female mosquito can sting. Male mosquitoes dine entirely on plant juices and nectar. The female pierces with her beak and not with a modified ovipositor, as does the bee or wasp. She has a mouth part which is like a knife with six sharp blades that fold together. She can even drill this into the tough skin of a frog or snake. When she bites, she injects a fluid which thins the blood of her victim and keeps it from clotting while she pumps it out. It also deadens the feeling of the victim very briefly. It is this irritating fluid that causes an itchy bump to appear on one's skin.

A female seeks blood because it is often needed for the production of fertile eggs. Most mosquitoes produce fewer eggs if they dine on human blood instead of animal blood. Outdoor life for humans would be much more pleasant if mosquitoes would realize this!

One common kind of mosquito lays her eggs in the form of a raft on the water. When the egg hatches, the larva is called a wriggler because of the way it travels. It is a tiny transparent creature that likes to hang upside down in the water while breathing through tubes located on the end of its body. The wriggler swims around head-over-heels to seek microscopic bits of plants and decaying matter. It takes this food in through a very efficient and unusual mouth arrangement. The wriggler's mouth has a pair of brushes, like mustaches, which it spreads apart to strain out food as it combs the water. Sometimes the wrigglers speed up the action of their brushes, using them as propellers to move faster.

When your shadow falls over the watery home of these larvae they will dive helter-skelter for the bottom. They pop up again very soon, for they must come up to breathe air.

When the larva has grown enough, it pupates. Most insect pupae are quiet and would seem to be dead, or at least sound asleep, if we did not know better. But the mosquito larva continues to lead a busy life. It splits its skin and the pupa, or tumbler, emerges. Now it resembles an ugly little insect gnome, with a big head and a hunched back and a slender abdomen, all in the shape of a comma. The tumbler dives for safety by lashing its tail-like abdomen back and forth. It does not eat during its three-

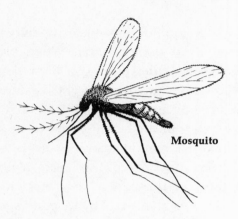

Mosquito

day pupal stage, but now it has developed an entirely new breathing arrangement. It takes in air at the surface of the water through a pair of tubes on its hunched back.

The water must be very still when the adult emerges from the pupal skin because a dousing now would be disastrous. When the pupa straightens out, it is a sign that the adult is ready for an air rather than a water environment. Air bubbles that have been carried under the pupal skin expand and some are also sucked into the mosquito's mouth. This helps to split the skin. Once the head is out of the skin, the mosquito pumps in more air, and is slowly and smoothly propelled up and out of its old shell. The long legs are withdrawn, and the adult either stands lightly on the surface of the water or uses the cast-off skin as a raft while it waits for its new wings to harden before flying off.

Some mosquitoes carry diseases, particularly mosquitoes that live in the southern hemispheres and in the tropics. Malaria and yellow fever can be extremely serious to humans. For this reason, many men have studied the life history of mosquitoes in hopes of learning how to control or banish them.

If you can overlook the mosquito's peskiness, you will find that there is much of interest happening during a mosquito's life cycle. The best way to find out is to raise some mosquitoes. You may find them if you keep a close watch for a couple of weeks on a rain barrel, a hole in a tree, or an old tin can full of water in the backyard.

Even though mosquitoes are pesky and some are disease carriers, they are an important source of food for other insects, birds, and fish. No one can predict exactly what would happen if they were all destroyed. It is very possible that the balance of nature would be upset and we could have greater problems than they now create for us.

CLICKS AND FLIPS

(Click Beetle)

You will have to search for the insect that makes one of the strangest sounds of all. It is the click beetle, or snapping bug. You will find it in the grass, in decaying wood, or under surface litter. It is a small, dull brown or black beetle. A very common

Click Beetle

woodland species has two large black eyelike spots on the forefront of its body.

You have probably noticed how often most beetles seem to fall on their backs in their clumsy, bungling way. They then paw the air frantically and helplessly for a while. However, the click beetle solves this upside-down problem in a special way. It has an unusual spine arrangement between the two sections of its body. First, it arches itself, and pulls out the section of spine on one part of its body. Then when it snaps forward the spine is jammed into place and the beetle flips into the air and usually lands on its feet. There is a loud "click" as it flips. Put the beetle on its back, wait as it plays dead for a while and then listen.

The larvae of the click beetles are the wireworms you find in the soil of the garden or under old pieces of wood. They are hard and thin; perhaps someone once thought that they were pieces of wire and named them that.

Insects make many other kinds of noises, too. For example, there is the "squeal" of the long-horned beetle when it is disturbed, the "pant" of a tired wasp, and the "crunch" of a feeding mantis or greedy caterpillar. Perhaps, too, insects make many meaningful sounds which our ears cannot hear.

You can listen to commercial recordings of insects' songs, sounds, and noises that can help you identify what you hear.

3

To Fly, Hop, or Crawl?

MOST INSECTS do not stand still long enough for you to look at them very carefully do they? Have you ever noticed how many different ways they use to get around? Many of them fly; others can jump or scuttle away very quickly. They move about in search of food, to find mates, or to escape from their enemies. Sometimes they must move to seek shelter from bad weather, such as wind, rain, or cold temperatures.

LONG DISTANCE FLIER

(Monarch Butterfly)

There's one flying insect that you are very likely to find sailing about in the air on a sunny summer day. It is not the fastest flier in the insect world or even the best; but it flies longer distances than almost any other, and it is probably our best-known butterfly. It is the bright orange and black monarch butterfly. A better name might be the All-American butterfly, for you can find monarchs from coast to coast. They are native to all of North America.

One of the most unusual things about this showy butterfly is the fact that it migrates each autumn from the North to the South and in the spring returns to the North. How and why the monarch does this is still partially a mystery to entomologists, just as the migration of birds is still not completely understood. The monarch is the best known migrating butterfly, but there are other kinds of butterflies that go South for the winter. Rarely do any of these make a round trip, though.

Many people have tried to trace the flight of monarchs by putting little tags on their wings. One monarch that was tagged and later found had flown almost 2,000 miles. It is difficult to believe that a butterfly's fragile, papery wings could carry it so far.

During the summer, in northern areas, the monarchs are born, mate, lay eggs, and die. However, some of those that emerge in late summer do not reproduce, but fly South to spend the winter. They do not fly in formation or in masses, as birds do, but occasionally a number may fly together in single file. Usually, they travel in twos or threes. At night they may come together to roost overnight in a tree.

They do gather in great numbers in some special areas after they finish the trip South. The city of Pacific Grove, California is known as Butterfly Town, U.S.A. because each autumn great swarms of monarchs roost together in the same grove of trees. They fly about during the day, sipping nectar, but they do not mate or lay eggs until they go North again the following spring.

They start their travel North when the milkweed begins to grow. The larvae of monarchs live almost exclusively on the common milkweed plant, so the females lay their eggs on milkweeds as they travel. When these hatch and the adults develop in the early spring, they also fly northward, sometimes to the very limit of milkweed growth. It may take as long as two months for an adult of the species to get from its southern winter home to as far north as Hudson Bay in Canada. The trip is made leisurely, because the adult only flies on bright sunny days. Although its body and wings are somewhat waterproof, it can become waterlogged in heavy rains, and be unable to fly.

The female monarch is rather selective about

her egg laying. She looks about to make sure that no predators are lurking nearby on the plant to feast on her babies. She never lays many eggs on any one milkweed. There are good reasons for this. By scattering her eggs about, the chance of survival of at least a few is better. Then, too, when the egg hatches in four or five days it is a very hard-working eating machine, gorging on milkweed leaves night and day. If more than one or two are on a plant, they soon eat themselves out of house and home.

In about two weeks, it grows from a tiny, pale green creature with a pin-sized, black head to a chubby, two-inch caterpillar with black, white and yellow stripes. If a human baby grew at the same rate, it would weigh several tons when it was a few weeks old.

The caterpillar has quite a number of legs, but there are two different kinds. It has the six true legs of an insect, but while it is in the caterpillar stage these are stubby and underdeveloped. They will become the six legs of the adult butterfly later. It also has five pairs of false legs which are called prolegs, and these are used for walking and crawling.

If a bird attacks the caterpillar, it will roll into a ball and drop down to the ground, concealing itself in grass or weeds. When the danger is past, it finds a milkweed plant again.

During the caterpillar's eating orgy, it will shed its skin several times. To help it get out of its old, tight covering, a fluid seeps between the old skin and the new. The layer of old skin dissolves and makes the new skin slippery enough for the insect to slide out. After it makes one last molt, the final magic transformation begins.

Now the caterpillar finds a twig or leaf and spins a small silk button. It holds on to this button, or pad, with its prolegs. It then loosens the grip of the prolegs one by one until it falls free, head down. The larva has a little spinelike stalk at the end of its body, and it must hook this stalk into the silk fastening pad. It twists and turns and writhes until the hook is secure and the old larval skin splits and is cast off. The larva appears to shrink, and then it is slowly encased in a lovely jade green shell with little gold-colored flecks, which is called a chrysalis. Butterflies do not spin silky cocoons, as many moths do. Instead, the butterfly pupa has a thin outer covering.

The chrysalis hangs quietly from several days to three weeks, depending on the weather. You can see very little on the outside, but inside great changes are taking place. Substances in the fluid of the body of the larva cause some old parts to break down and be absorbed, and new parts to be formed. The caterpillar loses some of its legs. The mouth disappears and becomes a tubelike structure, or proboscis, which is designed for sucking nectar. Wings develop and the reproductive organs form. When it is nearly time for the adult to emerge, the pupal case is almost transparent, and you can see the color of the developing wings.

Then one day a crack appears in the lower part of the case, and the adult monarch butterfly emerges. The soft, moist wings are crumpled and wrinkled. The butterfly hangs with its wings down, pumping fluid through the veins in the wings. The wings gradually unfold, dry out, and take shape. In time the veins, too, harden to form a framework for the wings. Soon it will fly off to search for nectar, water, and a mate.

A male monarch butterfly has one distinctive marking, a small black spot on the upper surface of each hind wing. These are hollow scent pockets containing specialized scales which produce an odor that attracts the female. The scent is too faint for humans to distinguish, but is is irresistible to a female monarch.

Monarch Butterfly

The monarch butterfly is not attractive to birds because of its disagreeable taste and odor. Their consumption of so much milkweed is what may make them so unappetizing. The bright orange and black coloring of the butterfly is a warning so that it will not be mistaken for a more tasty butterfly. Not all birds know this, and each season some monarchs are sacrificed.

The monarch butterfly has a smaller look-alike relative, the viceroy butterfly. The adult coloring and markings are so similar that you have to look closely to tell them apart. Scientists believe that the viceroy butterfly, which apparently tastes very good to birds and other predators, evolved into the monarch's close twin in appearance so that it would be mistaken for the bad-tasting monarch and be left alone. During the earlier stages of its life, however, it does not resemble the monarch at all.

The monarch has three pairs of legs, but only two pairs are used for walking. The front pair are shorter and fold against its body. The monarch, like other butterflies, tastes with its legs. Many can detect a faint amount of sweetness in a liquid that humans would not be able to taste.

When you pick up a butterfly, you will notice a little powdery substance on your hands. These are tiny scales that have come off its body and wings. Once the scales are lost they are never replaced. The scales are what give the butterfly wings their color. Some butterflies seem to be almost iridescent and shiny; others, such as the monarch, are a flat, bright color and do not shimmer in the light. The color of a butterfly is due to the effect of light hitting the scales that cover butterfly wings. The orange, red, and yellow colors usually come from transparent scales that are filled with a coloring matter that absorbs the light. This is called pigmented color. The butterflies with brilliant shiny blue, green, and violet coloring have scales that cause the light to bounce off and reflect only certain rays to our eyes.

Butterflies appear to be peaceful creatures, and you would not think that they had any desire for fighting. Actually, they do have battles now and then, but this is mostly bluff and bluster. They can buffet each other with their wings, and if they stay at it long enough, their wings will become frayed and torn.

Although monarchs are among our most common butterflies and can be found almost any place in the United States, they have good years and bad years, like other creatures. During a good year in a certain locality, there will be many of them around. In a bad year, weather and other environmental conditions may cut down the number that live to adulthood. It is possible, too, that there may not be as many in the future because of man's actions. As land is cleared for towns and fields, there is less milkweed left growing for the monarchs to feed on. Air pollution and the use of pesticides may also cut down on the number that survive. The All-

American butterfly may not be quite so plentiful in the years ahead.

THE HOP IN THE 'HOPPER

(Short-Horned Grasshopper)

Insect's legs may be well suited for walking, running, digging, swimming, or jumping. And for their size, insects are the most powerful jumpers of any creature.

One "olympic champion" jumper is the short-horned grasshopper. It can leap ten times its length in a standing broad jump. If man could do as well, he could jump over a five-story building or the length of a football field. Actually, the grasshopper's muscles are no more powerful for its weight than a man's, but the grasshopper's muscles just work more efficiently.

The grasshopper's large powerful hind legs are his jumping legs. He often squats with them held close to his body and with the "knee" above his body. He can walk at a slow gait, but when he does his hind legs take one step and his four short front ones must take two or more!

The grasshopper's jumps are controlled by a nerve signal system that is rather extraordinary. And how far he jumps depends on the number of impulses sent to his leg muscles along this system. One signal and he hops; two signals and he jumps a short distance; but three, and he goes all out! He

Short-Horned Grasshopper

can jump farther than he is able to see clearly, and he does not always choose the direction carefully when he is in a real hurry. And he usually jumps by zig-zags with his middle and front legs serving as his landing gear.

He uses his unusual back legs for something else. When he draws them across the thickened veins of the forewings, he can create grasshopper songs. Have you ever noticed the rattling noise he makes when he is in the air? He does this by vibrating the same hind legs against his wings.

A grasshopper can climb, as well as walk and jump. A sticky substance is released from pads on the bottom of his feet to help him go up, just as a repairman climbs a telephone pole with spurs on his feet.

There are many species of short-horned grasshoppers. They are related to the long-horned grasshoppers, such as the katydid; but the short-horns have sticklike antennae that are less than half the length of their bodies. Some of the short-horned grasshoppers are very, very destructive. They may migrate in great swarms, eating every green thing in their path. This is what people mean when they speak of a plague of locusts, for a locust is a migratory short-horned grasshopper.

Grasshoppers are a diet staple of many birds and small animals, so they have their problems, too. In fact, Aesop's fable about the grasshopper and the ant is really not fair to the grasshopper. It's true that some ants work hard, but not all are industrious and clean living, as the fable claims. Some are warriors and thieves. Music as well as hard work is important, and ants can't make any music as the grasshoppers can. Actually, the grasshopper is not a "ne'er-do-well" as Aesop said. True, he does not store up food for the winter; but, like many other adult insects, he has a short one-season life span. And the grasshopper provides for the survival of future generations of grasshoppers in its own way.

The female lays her eggs in the ground, and the small grasshoppers come out the following spring. First she makes a tunnel in the soil. She has three pointed prongs on the end of her body which she works back and forth like little shovels. At the bottom of the tunnel she has dug, she produces a froth in which she lays numerous eggs, each about the size of a grain of rice.

When the eggs hatch from the pod in the spring they are enveloped in a tough covering. The young grasshopper's body is very soft at this time, and the covering protects it from the rough soil as it struggles to climb out of the tunnel. The first one out has the hardest job, of course, and the rest can follow more easily. Once out of the ground the covering is cast off. The baby grasshopper looks like a miniature adult. It develops by incomplete metamorphosis and does not have to go through the caterpillar, or larval stage, as do many other insects. It just eats and grows and sheds its skin, and eats and grows and sheds again. In forty to sixty days it casts off its skin for the last time and is an adult grasshopper.

Have you ever caught a grasshopper in your hand and said, "Chew tobacco, chew tobacco; spit, spit, spit?" You know, then, that the grasshopper does spit out what looks like tobacco juice. This is an offensive foam that it discharges as a form of defense.

EXPERT DODGERS

(Leafhoppers)

Other fantastic jumpers of the insect world are members of a large group known as leafhoppers. They are small, slender creatures that come in a variety of colors. You might find one that is a light green, a brightly colored one called the red-banded, or a large blue one on the rosebush and other plants in the yard.

You will have to look carefully to find these fellows, even though there may be hundreds in the yard, because they have a trick of sliding quickly out

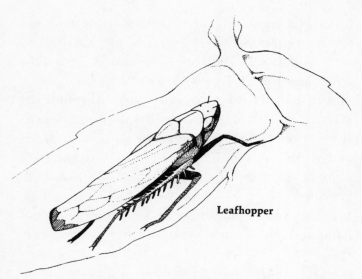

Leafhopper

of sight sideways around a leaf or stem. They are sometimes called dodgers because they dodge away so fast. The adults have wings and fly well, but they are more apt to use their powerful jumping legs and shoot into the air like a rocket. They can jump farther, for the size of their bodies, than the grasshoppers can.

They often hatch in grasslands during the spring from eggs laid the previous fall. Several generations may be born during the summer. A leafhopper lives about 40 days after hatching.

The leafhoppers are all sap suckers. In large numbers they may severely damage the plants on which they feed by sucking the sap and causing the plant to wilt. In a severe infestation, there may be as many as a million leafhoppers to an acre in a field

of crops. They also transmit virus diseases from
plant to plant and can be a serious pest to man.

TOO MANY LEGS?

(Daddy-Longlegs)

There's one creature you will find just walking
around leisurely in the summer that you probably
know by name; it's the daddy-longlegs. You have
surely noticed its long, gangling legs that are longer
in relation to its body size than any other creature
you have seen. Did you stop to count the number?
There are eight legs or, at least, there should be.
So, of course, it is no insect, but it is a relative of
the spider family.

Perhaps there were only seven or five legs on the
daddy-longlegs you found. That is because occasionally it may lose a leg. Like some other creatures,
including some insects, the daddy-longlegs can
grow new legs. A new leg will replace a lost one
when the creature molts, or casts off its old skeleton; the new leg replacement develops underneath
the old covering. But if it is an adult and will not
molt again, it cannot grow another leg.

The daddy-longlegs travels about with its body
low and its eight knees high above its head. The
eight legs are something like a fence around its
body. The second pair of legs are often extended
far out ahead to touch and explore the area. Sometimes it seems to be waving those two legs about.

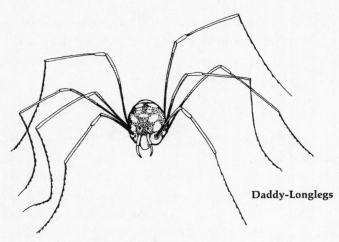

Daddy-Longlegs

The daddy-longlegs' body is small and rounded. Near the front are two stubs with an eye on each tip, one on the right and one on the left. It also has two protruding mouth parts in which it catches its prey as its body travels along close to the ground. It is protected from coming too close to dangerous insects partly by the "fence" of long legs around it and partly because it can give off a strong disagreeable odor from two scent glands at the base of the first pair of legs.

In many places the daddy-longlegs is known as the harvestman. Apparently this is because they seem to be numerous at harvest time. This really isn't a very good reason because many other insects are also most plentiful in late summer at harvest time, too. There is an old saying that if there are a lot of daddy-longlegs about, there will be a good harvest. This might have some basis in fact. The daddy-longlegs eat insects, especially aphids. If there are enough daddy-longlegs around, perhaps they do help to insure a good harvest by eating harmful insects.

SKATER'S WALTZ

(Water-Strider)

Water is a strange surface to walk on. If you go to a pond or the still backwaters of a lake, you will find one of the few creatures that has ever managed this feat with his feet. It is the water-strider.

These are bugs whose wings have almost disappeared through evolution. They do not fly away when disturbed, but skate or row away on the water at great speed. They use only four of their six legs to get about, and the four legs stay on the water's surface all the time, held far apart. The water-strider is supported by the surface tension of the water, which is strong enough to keep him from sinking. The water will sag under the insect's weight, and on a sunny day you can see the dimples or depressions in the water under each foot.

The feet of the water-strider are covered with fine hairs, and these act like snowshoes to keep them from breaking through the surface. There are claws on their feet, too; but they are located back from the end of the leg so that they do not pierce the water's surface. If the surface tension is broken for any reason, they will flounder.

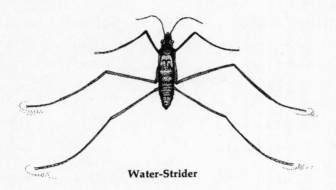

Water-Strider

The one pair of legs not on the water's surface is used to seize food. Water-striders feed on insects that fall into the water or that are found on vegetation growing in the water. You will often find great numbers of water-striders gathered together, darting here and there across the water in sudden spurts of activity.

A MINIATURE CATAPULT

(Springtail)

One insect cannot fly, and it's not well adjusted to walking. But it has a special forklike attachment at the end of its body that folds under its abdomen and is held in place by a catch. When it wants to move away it releases this attachment which then acts like a spring. The fork strikes the ground hard and the insect shoots off through the air, like a catapult. The insect is called a springtail.

They are very common, and there are many species; but you will need sharp eyes to find them, for they are small, often less than one-sixteenth of an inch in size. Nevertheless, they are very abundant, and you can find them in many dark, moist places, such as under logs, leaves, and stones. They may even be seen on the snow at times during a February thaw, looking like tiny black specks.

Springtails have another claim to fame, in addition to their unusual way of getting about. They are the most prevalent of the primitive insects, and one of the oldest known fossil insects. In other words, they have been around a long, long time. Their appearance has not changed much in all that time, and they are still very plentiful.

Scientists call an insect primitive when it is wingless and changes size, but not physical appearance, as it develops. There are some adult wingless insects that are not considered "primitive" though. That is because they once had wings and have lost them in the process of evolution. A true primitive insect never has had wings at any time in its known history.

Springtail

LOOP THE LOOP

(Measuring Worm; Geometrid Larva)

Have you been measured for new clothes lately? Maybe you have and did not know it! For there is an old superstition that you will get a new suit if the measuring worm crawls over you.

This is that little caterpillar that moves about in such a strange way that it seems to be measuring each step he takes. He lifts the front end of his body, thrusts it forward and then down to take hold with his front legs; then he draws his rear end up behind his front legs, making a loop of his body.

The measuring worm moves about this way because something is lacking. Most caterpillars have a number of prolegs, in addition to the six true legs. These extra, soft, stubby legs make it possible for the larva to cling to branches and other surfaces, as well as to crawl about more easily. These prolegs always disappear when the larva becomes an adult. The measuring worm has only two or three pairs of prolegs instead of the more numerous pairs that other insects have; so it cannot crawl very efficiently. Instead it gets ahead by looping the loop.

Some measuring worms may use their legs in another odd way. When disturbed or frightened, they will hold on to a branch with the back prolegs and extend their bodies out at an angle into the air. They may look exactly like a twig on the branch, and

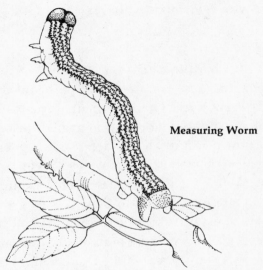

Measuring Worm

thus may be overlooked by a hungry bird. Other kinds will try to escape from danger by spinning a silk thread from their mouths and dropping down through the air some distance.

Measuring worms have other common names, such as loopers, inchworms, or cankerworms. There are about one thousand different kinds of measuring worms, and they are all larvae of the geometrid moths. Geometrid is derived from the Greek word *geometer* meaning earth measurer. The adults are rather undistinguished moths. You may find a number and variety around an outside light at night. The larvae of some are rather serious pests at times, because they feed upon the foliage of valuable trees and bushes.

THE STATIONARY SQUATTER

(Oystershell Scale)

It's hard to catch—or catch up— with many insects because they move so fast and in so many different ways. There is one that spends most of its life in one spot, not moving at all. It just may be the laziest insect of all. In fact, it uses its legs so little that as it matures, it may lose them completely.

At first glance, you may not have known that this was an insect, for it looks like a scaly growth on the skin of many fruits, tree twigs, and plant stems. This insect is known as the oystershell scale, and you can find it in most areas of the United States. You would probably overlook it entirely because it is so small except for the fact that it tends to live in large groups with other oystershell scales.

After the young insect is born, it wanders about

Oystershell Scales

for a few days. Then it drives its beak down into a plant and spends the rest of its life in that one spot. It covers itself with a waxy substance, and under this protective wax scale it will eat, lay eggs, and eventually die.

The oystershell scale has many scale relatives, such as mealy bugs and the San Jose scale, but none are looked upon with much favor by anything but titmice, chickadees and some other birds who thoroughly enjoy them as a staple in their diet. However, a certain kind of scale insect produces a substance called "lac" from which shellac is made. And various useful dyes and waxes are made from the scales of others.

Will it fly, jump, walk, or stand still all its life? Insects have various interesting ways of getting around. The main reasons for moving about are to get food and to escape from enemies; but often they must also be able to find mates, suitable places to lay their eggs, and a place to hibernate, if that is part of their life process. And to do all this, some have developed very specialized limbs and various appendages. Man has his arms and legs which he can use in many ways, but instead of growing wings or extra legs, he has developed wheels, airplanes, and other mechanical devices for moving about in all the ways that insects can and more. Insects can only move in the same manner that their parents did, with what they grow themselves.

4

Night Adventures

YOU CAN go insect hunting at night, also. If you leave an outside light burning on a still night, there will soon be quite a crowd of insects flying about it. During different times of the year you will see different kinds of insects.

Why are various insects attracted to the light? Some insects, such as certain moths, react to light of particular intensities by keeping their bodies turned at an angle so that the amount of light in each eye is equal. This causes them to fly directly toward the source of light, even right into it. This attraction to light is called phototropism. Insects respond to light in may ways, not all of which are understood by scientists yet. The intensity of the light has a different effect on different insects. For example, butterflies are attracted by brilliant sunlight, but moths are repelled by it. Insects that respond to daylight are seldom attracted by artificial light. Various insects also respond to the wave lengths of light in different ways. The short wave lengths of blue and ultra-violet seem to appeal to many insects.

BUMBLING BUG

(May Beetle)

Early in the summer you will hear the clumsy, dark-colored June bug going bump in the night near the light. It is not a very good flier and often ends up with a thud against a window screen or wall. The June bug, as most people call him, is really more properly called a May beetle, for he is not a bug at all.

The May beetle is only active at night, and during the day it hides in the grass or in the ground. You will only find May beetles bumping around when the temperature is at least 60° F. They do not operate very well when it is colder than that. Body temperatures of beetles and other insects are not regulated as warm-blooded animals' body temperatures are.

The May beetle you find may have spent three

years as a white grub, which is a larva that lives in the ground feeding on roots. You can often find them digging in the lawn or other grassy areas. During the summer they gradually dig deeper into the dirt, build a little earthen chamber around themselves, and pupate. In a few weeks, the adult beetle emerges, but it stays in the ground below the frost line and is protected from the cold winter, until the following spring.

When the May beetle comes above ground it feeds and mates. Then the female lays her eggs in the center of a ball of earth, which she sticks together with a substance from her body.

The May beetle has an enemy, a fly with a vicious habit. This fly hovers around until the May beetle

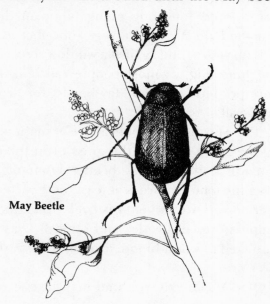

May Beetle

is flying. Then it strikes. When the beetle is flying, the hard wing covers are raised up and out of the way, and the beetle's tender back is exposed. The fly darts in, jabs the beetle's back, and inserts its own eggs in the beetle's body. In a few days the fly's eggs hatch, and the fly larvae feed on the beetle's live body. Soon the beetle is dead.

The life cycle of this parasitic fly is annual, for it hatches, mates, and lays its eggs all in one season. Most May beetles take three years in the northern United States or two years in the southern portion to do all this. And then they spend most of their time underground. So if it is a year when there are few adult May beetles out and about, the flies themselves may almost die off for lack of a beetle's back in which to lay their eggs.

A May beetle's center of gravity seems to be a little off-center, for when the beetle falls, it almost always seems to land on its back. Then there is a great thrashing and kicking of legs until it manages to get upright again.

The May beetle has a close relative which is called the Green June bug, or figeater. This is a pretty shiny beetle that is more commonly found in the southern United States. The larva eats underground, like the May beetle larva, and the adult feeds on the leaves and fruit of orchard and garden plants, including figs when they are available. The larva has one peculiar habit. It moves about by wriggling on its back.

You will find many other kinds of beetles out at night. In fact, you will find beetles all over, day or night, in many different places. There are thousands of different species of beetles in the United States and many, many more in other parts of the world. In fact, beetles form the largest single order in the entire animal kingdom.

THE BEETLE WITH HORNS

(Stag Beetle)

One of the strangest looking beetles you may find under the porch light is the stag beetle. This is a shiny hard-shelled beetle with enormous pincer jaws that look like antlers. You may even find two males battling over a female and jousting with these hornlike jaws. Stag beetles are often found in large colonies in rotten logs. They are sometimes called pinching bugs. It's the kind of beetle that Mark Twain's Tom Sawyer took to church one Sunday.

Stag Beetle

Beetles are very strong insects for their size. One stag beetle was harnessed in an experiment and pulled 120 times its own weight. The average insect can drag about twenty times its own weight, but the average person can usually move something that only weighs as much as he does. The muscles of all insects have great leverage and powers of endurance, but there are other differences that make such comparisons difficult or inaccurate.

WINGS WITH EYES

(Polyphemus Moth)

In late May or early June you may have a very different kind of visitor attracted to a light at night. It will be the polyphemus moth, which is named after Polyphemus, the one-eyed giant Greek god. Its name is a clue to one of its distinctive features, the large eye spot on each hind wing.

Some other moths also have eyespots, but the polyphemus is the largest with a wingspan that is often five to six inches across. The distinct oval eye spots have transparent centers with blue and black bands encircling them. These spots may be a protective device for the moth. Perhaps they tend to frighten away a bird when it suddenly sees what appears to be two large staring eyes. Or the eye spots may distract the bird from attacking the more vital parts of the moth's body.

The polyphemus moth is a native of North

America and can be found almost any place in the United States. During the feeding stage of its life it eats a wide variety of leaves, unlike those insects which are restricted to just one or two varieties of plants, such as the monarch butterfly. This means that the polyphemus can live almost any place, although it is especially fond of oak, elm, maple and birch leaves.

The adult moth that you find attracted to the light does not eat at all. It will live only a few days, just long enough for mating and for the female to lay eggs. The female releases a very delicate perfume in the air as she flies about. The male may pick up this scent from several miles away. He has special organs on his long plumelike antennae that give him this remarkable sense of smell.

The female lays her eggs in clusters on leaves. The eggs are small, round, and a creamy color with an edging of brown. In about ten or twelve days the caterpillar emerges from the egg and starts the cycle of eating-and-molting, eating-and-molting. The caterpillar turns a bright green, with red spots on its body and silvery stripes and tufted spines on its back.

It manages to look very fierce when disturbed by rearing up and drawing its head back and clicking its jaws! When it is busy feeding you may actually be able to hear the jaws click as it munches away.

It will shed its skin several times as it gets bigger. After about a month and a half of uninterrupted eating, with its appetite satisfied it is ready to spin its cocoon and start the next stage of its life. This stage will last longer than any of the other cycles in its life, for in most parts of the country it will stay encased in the cocoon over the winter. It wraps itself in some leaves and spins out the cocoon in one continuous silk thread, perhaps as much as a mile and a half of it. The polyphemus is a silk moth and related to the silkworms that are raised to produce the silk that goes into cloth.

The cocoons of the polyphemus may be difficult to find because they are a drab brownish color with dead leaf particles attached. They often fall to the ground in the winter where their color blends in with the dead leaves littered under trees.

In early spring of the next year the cycle is completed as the adult moth emerges from the cocoon. First, a fluid is secreted that softens the silk threads of the cocoon so that they can be pushed aside with the moth's head. When it emerges, it is a wet and wrinkled mass that certainly doesn't look too attractive. It must immediately climb upward so that gravity will help to pull out its unfolding wings.

If for any reason its wings do not unfold completely during this drying out and hardening period, it will not be able to fly. The weather in late May or early June is not always predictable. And if,

Polyphemus Moth

for the brief days of its adult life the weather is
windy, cold, and rainy, the moth may not be able
to fly about much or even leave its first perch. In
that case, it may die without ever mating.

Moths and butterflies belong to the order Lepidoptera which means scale wings. If you handle a
polyphemus, you will get the same kind of dustlike
particles on your hands that come off of a butterfly's
wings. It is not always easy to tell moths and butterflies apart, although there are certain general differences. The ones that fly about during the day are
usually butterflies; moths usually fly at night. If the
insect's wings are out flat when it is resting, it most
likely is a moth, although some fold their wings like

a tent over their bodies. Butterflies usually hold their wings upright after they light.

The antennae are another clue as to which is which. The antennae of most butterflies are slender, with a knob on the end. A moth's antennae are usually feathery, and seldom have knobs. The delicate antennae of the polyphemus, for example, are like soft brown plumes.

There is a hairy, almost furry covering on the moth's plump body. The monarch butterfly does not have any such covering on its body. This fuzziness on the body is another way to help distinguish moths and butterflies.

The caterpillars of both moths and butterflies come in such a wide variety of sizes and shapes that it is hard to tell which is which at this stage. When the caterpillar retires to make its transformation you can make a better guess as to what it is. A butterfly larva makes a naked pupa, or chrysalis, and affixes it to a support for its changing chamber. If you find a drab cocoon with a silky or hairy covering, whether hanging from a branch or on the ground, it may be a moth. At least, it is more likely to be a moth than a butterfly!

There are many more kinds of moths in North America than butterflies. The larval forms of some moths are extremely destructive, and cause millions of dollars of damage to crops, clothes, and carpets. However, few butterflies are any bother to man.

FLYING DADDY-LONGLEGS

(Crane Fly)

One of the insects that you are likely to find near the porch light at night looks like a giant mosquito with extra long legs. Don't swat it! This is a crane fly, and it does not bite man at all, despite its close resemblance to the pesky mosquito.

It gets its name from its legs, which resemble those of a crane. And like the daddly-longlegs, the legs are easily broken off, too. It is very hard to find one with its legs intact. If you capture one, you will be able to see the fly's halteres, or balancing organs, behind each wing. The organs are larger and more prominent than in most flies. These are the structures that have replaced the second pair of wings in all true flies.

Crane flies live in damp places; and some kinds lay their eggs in water. The larvae of others are known as leather jackets because they are so tough

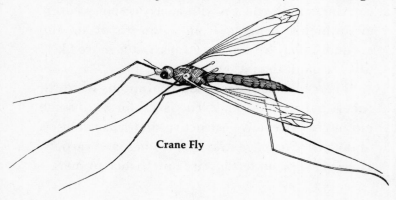

Crane Fly

and leathery. In early spring or fall you may find swarms of crane flies doing a wild dance just a few feet above the surface of wet areas. Fishermen often tie bits of feathers together to resemble crane flies and use these to catch trout or other stream fish.

LANTERNS IN THE DARK

(Firefly)

You won't need an outside light to find one summer night flyer. The firefly, or lightning bug, carries its own light around, turning it off and on in a regular pattern. Sometimes an entire field, lawn, or woods will be twinkling with hundreds of these little "lanterns." It is not hard to catch fireflies, for they are slow moving and give themselves away with their flashes. At first glance, close-up or in the daytime, a firefly is disappointing to look at, for it is a drab little creature. But then it performs its amazing act of lighting up and seems anything but drab.

There are several common kinds of fireflies in the United States. They operate on different time schedules. The one you find in your area may fly about only from dusk until the last glow of the sun has left the sky, and they will be active only for a few weeks in early summer. They stay fairly close to the ground and the males flash a single yellowish light at average intervals of six seconds. They flash more often if it is a hot night and less often if it is cooler. They fly in an up and down manner, and always flash on the upswing. They look like little sparks shooting up from the ground. The female stays in the grass and answers the male with a fainter flash, which she turns on two seconds after she sees the male's signal. You can try luring in a male by putting a flashlight on the ground. Turn it on and then off two seconds after you see a flash in the air nearby. The male may descend to the light.

Other kinds of fireflies flash their lights in different ways. One kind gives two short flashes at a time, and a high-flying species may flash as many as five times in rapid succession and be answered by two or three flashes from the female on the grass. Some stop flashing early in the evening; others will continue until midnight or a short time later.

There are fireflies in many parts of the world; some shine much more brilliantly than ours do. In some areas their light is so bright that a number of them gathered in a glass bottle will make a very useful lantern or lamp to read by. In Thailand and Burma thousands of fireflies gather on certain trees, and together they soon begin to flash their lights on and off. It is like watching lightning coming from trees.

When you hold a firefly in your hand, he seems to glow constantly. Then he will "flash" briefly. But his flashes will probably not be in the same pattern if he has been injured in any way. Then his flashes may be almost constant, as if his regulator was out of order.

Why does a firefly light up? One reason seems to be to find a mate. Unlike most insects, fireflies are attracted by light rather than scent or sound, and the flash is a signal between the male and female. But some kinds do not flash when they are adults at all; they glow only in the larval stages.

A firefly that shines from the ground may be a glowworm, which is a wingless female or a larva. The eggs of some kinds of fireflies also glow, which doesn't seem to have any particular use at all.

The firefly's light does not help it to see where it is going, for it carries its lantern near its posterior. And it is certainly no protection against its enemies, for it is easier to see in the dark. In fact, some frogs have eaten so many lightning bugs that their stomachs shine, as if they had swallowed a light bulb.

There are many other mysteries about fireflies that have not been completely solved yet. For many years scientists worked to unlock the puzzle of just what the firefly's light really was. They knew it was a "cold" light. That means there was no heat generated from the light as there is from a light bulb, a candle, or the sun. They knew it was an efficient kind of light, too, for that reason. No energy was wasted, as in most lights, by generating useless heat.

The light in the common adult male firefly comes from the underside of its body where there is a transparent membrane. A special organ in the firefly's body produces a protein called luciferin. An

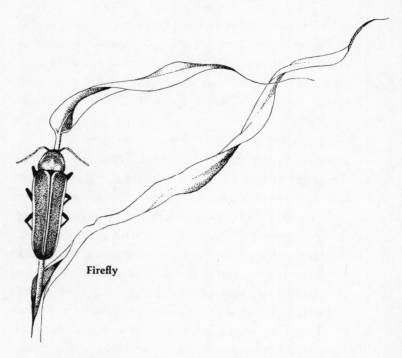

Firefly

enzyme called luciferase is also present. When the
insect draws air into its body the luciferin and oxygen are mixed in the presence of the luciferase. As
the luciferin molecules burn up, they produce the
cold and silent light flash. There are no infrared or
ultra-violet rays in the firefly's light. The light from
a fluorescent lamp most closely resembles the light
of a firefly.

The firefly, or lightning bug, is neither a fly nor
a bug. It is a beetle. There are two wing cases on
the firefly's back which are lifted up and out of the

way of the second pair of wings when it flies, like most beetles.

The female in some species has wings, although she seldom flies, and in other species she has no wings at all. She is usually slightly larger than the male. She lays as many as 200 eggs in damp soil, which hatch out in about three weeks.

The larvae live in and on the ground, and feed at night on such small creatures as slugs, snails, aphids and soft-bodied insects. They do not feed on plants. The larvae have two sharp little prongs on their jaws which they use to inject a paralyzing poison into their victims. Although their victims may be quite a bit larger than they are, the poison turns flesh or body organs into a soupy substance which the larva can then suck up.

The larvae may be difficult to find unless you search hard, but they are intriguing to watch. Besides, there is an old saying that you will have brilliant success in an undertaking if a glowworm appears in your path!

You will find many odd insects about when you search them out at night. And it is the only time you will find some because they are only active after dark.

5

Live-Game Hunters

WHILE YOU are hunting for insects to observe, many of them are very busy hunting for other insects. In fact, insects are their own worst enemies. Many are predacious, which means they feed on other live insects. This constant state of warfare helps to keep the insect population in balance.

The live-game hunters use many methods to locate and capture their prey. They may seize their victims in midair, rush them on the ground, or hide and wait until a juicy morsel comes within reach.

THE HOLY TERROR

(Praying Mantis)

With sharp eyes and a little patience you may be able to locate one of the greediest insects of all, the praying mantis. There are several different kinds in the United States, although there is only one kind that is native. Others have come to this country from other parts of the world. This was accidental at first, as they came into the United States on plants imported from Europe and Asia. Now they are often colonized and shipped about the country to aid gardeners in controlling insect pests.

A praying mantis is so distinctive in appearance that once you have found one, you will know what it is. The kind you are most likely to find in late summer may be as much as four or five inches long, one of our largest insects, and green or brownish in color. And at that time of the year its appetite is simply tremendous. It will eat friend and foe alike; it will even eat another mantis.

The name praying mantis is almost a pun. When it is at rest or waiting for a victim, which is most of the time, it perches on a twig or branch and is supported by its four back legs. Its body appears to be hinged in the middle, and the forepart is held upright. Its two front legs, attached to the "hinged" section, are raised high and folded under, as if it might be preparing to pray. But a better name

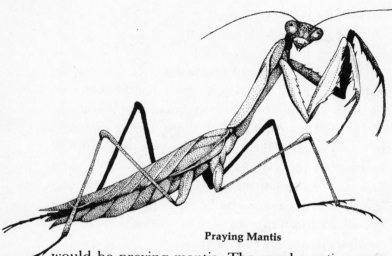

Praying Mantis

would be preying mantis. The word *mantis* comes
from the Greek word meaning prophet or sooth-
sayer, and it is suitable because the insect looks so
alert and full of secrets. The mantis holds its long
front legs up, not to pray, but to be ready to flash
out and seize any insect that comes close. Despite
the fact that it is an eager eater, it will not bite
humans. In fact, mantises make interesting pets.

The color and odd shape of the mantis' body
make it hard to be seen, particularly by another
insect. However, the mantis can see very well. It has
large eyes and keen vision. It can even turn its head
around and look over its shoulder, something no
other insect can do.

The front legs of the mantis are quite remarkable. They are not used for walking, but are adapted
for catching the mantis' victims. The long forelegs

have spikes on them. The legs open out suddenly, and the mantis grabs its prey between the two spined sections of its forelegs which are like a strong vise. Then it brings the insect up to its mouth. It always devours its prey in the same way, by biting the insect behind its head and cutting its main nerve. The mantis then cuts up its food with a set of structures that are like teeth, but these chop and grind sideways, rather than up and down.

After a hearty meal, you will see a mantis clean its spines and wash its face. Perhaps you have noticed that other insects, too, seem constantly to be cleaning themselves. The reason for this is more nearly like the reason that a man polishes his eye glasses than like the reason for washing one's hands. The sense organs of insects are located in many odd places, such as on their legs or on their antennae. If the insect is to feel, hear, or smell through these organs, they must be cleaned off frequently.

The mantis is very dangerous to other insects, but he has only one defense himself against other creatures. He can emit a liquid that has a very disagreeable odor. It may not be particularly offensive to man, but insects and other creatures have a much more delicate sense of smell, and the mantis' odor may be as bad to them as a skunk's is to us.

Although mantises are closely related to grasshoppers and crickets, which are plant eaters, mantises eat only live game. And they eat great quantities of it. They are so greedy that they have been known to strike at another victim while still stuffing down the remains of one just caught. In late summer, after mating, the female may even devour her mate. There are a few other insects and spiders that do this. Scientists believe this is an instinct that dates back to the time when food may have been in short supply and in great demand. After the male had served his purpose he was killed so that there was less competition for the available food.

The female lays her eggs in a case attached to a tree branch a few feet above the ground. She hangs head down and squeezes out a frothy substance from the tip of her abdomen. While the froth is still soft, she shapes it into an egg case. Then she lays eggs inside the mass, sometimes laying as many as 300. The case hardens rapidly and eventually turns dark brown.

The egg case hangs from its support during the winter, and in the spring it softens up. Soon the young mantises emerge from this spongy mass, and they seem to disappear completely, for they scatter quickly and are tiny and inconspicuous. Even at this young age, they are rearing up and assuming their praying pose.

Ants are enemies of mantises, and hordes of them may wait to attack the young mantises as they come out of their case. But the young mantises will eat each other, too; so it takes some fast footwork to get away and survive. If the mantises can avoid their enemies, by late summer they will be fully grown and busy eating every live insect within their reach.

FLYING BASKET TRAPS

(Dragonfly)

Another live-game hunter with a tremendous appetite is the dragonfly. They are often abundant near water, where they spend part of their life cycle. But you will find them on hunting flights over fields and trees, as well as near the water's edge.

Unlike the stealthy, slow-moving mantis, this hunter really gets around. It is on the wing almost constantly in good weather, and it has been clocked at flying speeds of up to sixty miles per hour. It can twist, swerve, fly straight up, hover, even fly backwards in midair.

The dragonfly is the most powerful insect flier of all. Its wings work in pairs, but the fore wings and back wings are not hooked together as they are in other insects. The fore wings beat down as the back wings come up, and this is timed so that there is relatively little turbulence created to hinder its wing movement. It also has a unique muscle movement. Most insects move their wings by flexing or arching the part of the body that the wings are attached to, but the dragonfly has a set of muscles attached di-

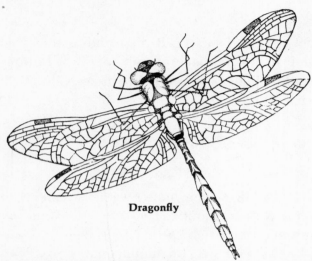

Dragonfly

rectly to the wing base which can be used to force
the wings down.

The dragonfly is not a true fly, of course, because he has four wings. They are transparent, but
seem to shimmer and flash in the sun, like bits of
cellophane. Some kinds are very brilliantly colored.

It can zero in on its target on the wing. Its main
interest is in other flying insects, primarily mosquitoes, which it consumes in great quantities.
Watch a dragonfly in action; you may be able to see
how it approaches its prey from below in a surprise
attack. Its legs are spiny, and it holds them together
in the shape of a small basket. Victims are scooped
up in this basket trap. It usually takes only moving
prey, but if you capture one, it will eat almost anything that you put into its mouth. It may consume
its own weight in food in a few hours.

A dragonfly's vision is very sharp, and he can see moving objects many feet away. Insects do not "see" the same way that humans do. The adult dragonfly, for example, has a large eye that bulges out. In each eye there are as many as 30,000 little lenses closely packed together, each of which transmits its own image. Thus it sees hundreds of little images all at the same time, which makes a pattern rather than a single picture. Insects sleep with their eyes open, for they have no way of closing them.

The dragonfly is relatively safe from birds because it can often outmaneuver them at short range. Each kind of dragonfly has its own flight habit. Some stay high in the air most of the time, and others may skim along only an inch or so above the water. The males often establish territories at mating time, as many birds do. Then they will guard their own territory fiercely, and try to drive off any intruders. You can actually hear the clash of wings when this happens. Despite this ferocious behavior, the dragonfly does not have much fighting equipment. It can't sting, and it most certainly can't sew one's ears together, as people once believed! One of its common names, devil's darning needle, or darner, comes from this old, false belief. Another common nickname is mosquito hawk and that is much more appropriate, since it preys upon mosquitoes constantly.

Dragonflies have been around for a very long

time. Fossils of dragonflies have been found that are millions of years old. Some scientists think that they are the first living creatures that could fly. At one time they were big enough to earn the name dragon. Small for dragons, perhaps, but very big for an insect; fossil dragonflies have been found with a wing span of two feet.

You often see dragonflies flying in tandem, one on top of the other. This is a mating flight, and the male sperm is transferred to the female's body in midair. Some females lay their eggs by dropping them freely on the water, and others cement the eggs to water plants. The male often accompanies the female on these egg-laying flights, sometimes still in tandem.

The young hatch out in late summer and spend the winter underwater. At this stage, they are called naiads and are quite ferocious looking. The naiad may have a lower lip that is as long as its body and folds under the upper lip. Up close this looks like a mask with a grotesque smile. It is no laughing matter for the dragonfly naiad's prey, though, for this lower lip is hinged in such a way that it can shoot out with lightning speed and grab a victim with two clawlike structures on the end of its lip. When the lip is pulled back it serves as a bowl to hold the food while it is consumed. The naiad eats other small water creatures, and it particularly fancies mosquito wigglers which it eats by the score. Large naiads can even attack tadpoles or little fish.

The naiad breathes by taking in water at the end of its body and then forcing it out. The insect crawls about on the bottom of a pond or stream on its legs, but if it is in a real hurry, it expels the water with greater force. Then it moves like an underwater rocket, jet-propelled, with its legs acting as oars.

Most dragonfly naiads spend the winter in the water, and then on a warm day in late spring they will crawl out of the water onto a rock, plant stem, or dry log. There they undergo one final molt, casting off their nymphal skin. After this struggle, which may take more than an hour, the body of the winged adult expands, the wings unfold and harden, and it is off for its final life phase in the air. Sometimes you can find dozens of cast-off skins near the water. If you happen to arrive at the scene in time to witness the emergence of the adults, you can see, first hand, how chancy this whole operation is. If the naiad is touched or disturbed in any way during the process, it seems to "freeze" at that point and all development stops.

Perhaps instead of dragonflies you will find their very close relatives, damselflies. They look and act so much alike that most people assume they are the same. Some mistakenly think that damselflies, which are smaller and more delicate than dragonflies, are just dragonflies growing up. The best way to tell them apart is to wait until they are at rest. The dragonfly clings to a support with its wings outstretched; the damselfly holds its wings upright over its back. And there's another slight difference, too. The back wings of the dragonfly are slightly broader than its fore wings. In the damselfly, the two pairs are about the same size. Damselflies are not as vigorous or as powerful as dragonflies either.

THE "ELEPHANT" HUNTER

(Cicada-Killer)

There's one big game hunter that goes after prey that may be four times larger than the hunter. This is a very large wasp called a cicada-killer. The female cicada-killer is very fussy about her game; she not only hunts only one kind of insect, but she hunts only the male. She does not eat the male cicada herself, but uses it to stock her nursery. She only sucks nectar or fermented tree sap for herself.

The cicada-killer is a solitary hunting wasp. It is sometimes called a king hornet because of its size, which may be up to two inches long. It is black and banded with yellow; the wings have a golden sheen. And it has a long, powerful stinger. It is quite formidable looking, but it is mainly interested in cicadas and practically never stings man.

Although it belongs to the same big family as the hornets, it is more closely related to the mud-dauber wasp. Cicada-killers do not live in colonies, as hornets and many other wasps do. You may see groups of them in the same area, but they do not work together.

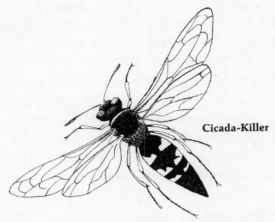

Cicada-Killer

Before setting off on her hunt, the female cicada-killer digs a deep burrow in the ground with a special room at the bottom. She digs and drags the dirt out backwards, clasped in her front legs, until her hole is several feet deep. Then she is ready to seek out the special game she wants.

It is not difficult for her to locate the particular insect she seeks. The male cicada is usually perched in a tree nearby, advertising his presence with his loud, continuous whirring or drumming.

The cicada-killer darts at him, and jabs her stinger into his nerve center. Sometimes there is a loud scream from the cicada. The two often fall to the ground during this flurry. Her sting paralyzes the male; he is alive, but unconscious and helpless. If they have tumbled to the ground during the attack, the wasp now has a problem. She must transport her prize to her burrow, but the cicada is much larger and heavier than she is. She does not have

enough strength to fly up into the air and proceed
to her nest with this burden. And it is difficult to
drag the victim a long distance to the burrow. Instead she will tug and haul the cicada up a tree trunk
until she is a few feet above the ground. Then she
grasps the cicada between her legs and takes off in
a long gliding flight toward her burrow. If she is a
long way from the burrow, she may not make it the
first time and will climb up another tree again and
take off on another flight.

Once she reaches the entrance to her nest, she
drags the cicada down into the prepared chamber
and lays an egg on its body. The egg will hatch into
a tiny white larva which feeds on the cicada, almost
entirely consuming it in about two weeks time.
Then the larva makes a cocoon, and spends the
winter underground in a dormant state as a pupa.
During the summer the young adult will dig its way
out of the ground, and if it is a female, she will
promptly start hunting the elephant-sized game.

FLYING SPEAR

(Ichneumon)

If you ever find an insect that appears to be
stinging a piece of wood, you may think that it is a
bit mixed up. But it knows exactly what it is doing
and why. It is a long-tailed ichneumon, one of a very
large and important group of insects that belongs

to the same family as wasps and bees. Strangely enough, they do not have any common names, but are simply called ichneumon or ichneumon wasps or sometimes ichneumonflies.

Most of them do not have any stingers; instead they have extremely long ovipositors which may be several times the length of their own bodies. They differ from the true wasps because their ovipositors extend from the underside of the abdomen instead of from its tip and are usually used for laying eggs. They do look very dangerous, but if you catch one and it attempts to sting with its ovipositor, you will scarcely feel it.

Members of this family do some very odd things, although it may be difficult to see them in action. They may be attracted to lights at night, or be found feeding on the nectar of flowers.

As a group they are important because they are all parasites. At some time in their life cycle they live on another insect and thus destroy it. They them-

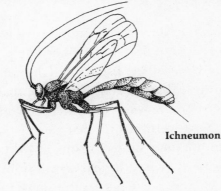

Ichneumon

selves are abundant, and by destroying other insects, they help to keep the numbers of undesirable ones in check. Therefore, they are an important natural control. There are many members of this family, but there may be even more to be named and described by entomologists in the future.

The one that you find "stinging" a piece of wood may very well be a contender for the honor of having the keenest sense of smell of any insect. She has located the larva of a wood-boring insect which may be an inch or more under the solid surface of the wood. She drills directly down and lays her eggs on the body of the larva. The ovipositor is hairlike, and it is difficult to understand how she can manage to drill through solid wood with it. Sometimes she gets it stuck in the wood, and if she cannot release herself, she is doomed.

AN EFFICIENT PIT-DIGGER

(Ant-Lion)

Have you ever noticed a number of little circular pits in an area of dry sand or loose dust? These are traps set by another insect game hunter. We have seen hunters that stalked their prey, that zeroed in on victims on the wing, or drilled down into hiding places. Now we find one that digs a pit and then waits until a juicy morsel drops in for dinner.

This pit digger is the larval ant-lion. The adult female scatters her eggs on the sandy soil surface, and when an egg hatches, the larva promptly digs into the soil and spends two or three years in this stage of its complete metamorphosis. Its larval body is covered with bristles and its head is shaped like a spade that has two hollow claws attached.

The larva always walks backward, but it manages some amazing feats even with this handicap. It can build a cone-shaped pit by shuffling around backward in a circle. It will shove its head into the sand, flipping and tossing grains up and away. It can even toss a small pebble out of its path, if necessary. When the pit is the right size, the ant-lion burrows under at the bottom with only its head and claws above the surface.

After constructing the pit, it will patiently wait for an ant or other small insect to tumble over the edge and slide down toward the center of the pit. If the ant-lion cannot grab it immediately, it throws grains of sand to create a miniature landslide. Then it seizes the victim with its long jaws and injects a poison that kills the victim and softens the tissues at the same time. After sucking the juices out of the victim's body, it flips the empty carcass away.

The larval ant-lion has a rather uncertain food supply. If its trap is not made near a busy insect intersection, it may have to wait days before a victim comes along. When the food supply is limited it will not grow very rapidly.

As the ant-lion larva grows, it builds bigger and bigger pits. Some pits may be more than two inches

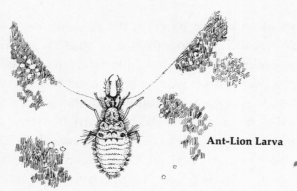

Ant-Lion Larva

across and an inch or more deep. If you shove a little sand down the edge of a pit with a twig or blade of grass, you may trigger a geyser of grains from the bottom of the pit because the ant-lion will foolishly think that some victim has fallen into its trap.

The ant-lion eventually makes a cocoon underground. This is a hollow ball of sand cemented together and lined with silken threads. It is mysterious the way the ant-lion manages to construct the sand ball and not get one grain of sand inside it!

A month or two later, the adult lacy-winged ant-lion struggles up out of the sand and flies away. It has a short life, living only a few weeks.

TIGER TRAPS

(Tiger Beetle)

The ant-lion sets its trap in soft or sandy soil, but you will find another hunter lying in wait for its victims in many different places. This is the tiger beetle, and the larval tiger beetle makes its trap in the middle of a path in the woods, bare rocky soil, sandy beaches, grassy roadsides, or hard dry dirt.

Adult tiger beetles come in an assortment of colors. Some are bright blue, green, purple, or brown. Others have metallic-colored stripes, and these stripes suggest the name tiger. It's blood-thirsty enough to have earned the name, too.

A tiger beetle is an oddity in its larval stage. It builds a trap by making a deep vertical hole in the ground. This shaft is often about the size of a lead pencil. The larva backs down into the hole and covers the opening with its head, like a lid. It, too, is a patient hunter, and waits until a victim wanders near. Then it shoots its head out and grabs the prey. Rarely will this larva leave the burrow, by choice or by force.

Its head is very large in proportion to the rest of its body. The hard, flat head is almost at a right angle to the body and equipped with a set of powerful jaws. The rest of the body is soft and unprotected. But on the middle of its back there is a small hump with a pair of stout hooks which help the tiger beetle larva to move up and down inside its burrow. It also can dig the hooks into the burrow walls to guard against being dragged out by a large and powerful victim.

After a year or so, the larva will close up the

Tiger Beetle Larva

burrow's entrance and pupate. When the adult tiger beetle emerges, it has a large body with long legs. This swift-moving beetle is very difficult to catch and may run a few feet or fly a short distance if you approach it. The adult continues to be a live-game hunter; but now it runs down its food, instead of lying in wait for it. It catches insects in its clawlike jaws. Be careful when handling one because it can give you a painful bite.

Not all of the live-game hunters we have found seek out just insects that we consider destructive or harmful, but all help to keep the total insect population in check. This is a form of biological control.

Man tries to use biological control, too, to destroy or cut down on the numbers of certain insects. Many of our worst pests are not native to this country, but have come from other parts of the world. Often the insects which also keep them from overpopulating do not come along with the pests. Then entomologists may attempt to find and import the parasites or predators that will attack them. In some instances this has been very successful, and in others it has not.

Man has used many methods in an attempt to control or destroy insect and animal populations. Both intentionally and unintentionally, he has completely destroyed some birds and animals, so that they are now extinct. But in all history, as far as we know, he has never been able to eliminate a single insect species. Now we are learning more about the interrelationships and interdependence of all living things in our environment. We know that we must be careful in our efforts to control or destroy. If not, the results may be unpredictable and possibly very unpleasant or dangerous to all living creatures. Even the lowly mosquito, annoying as he is, may play an important role in the balance of nature.

6
Masquerades

WHEN YOU go to a Halloween party or a masquerade, you may dress up to look like something else. If you dress like a ghost, a witch, or a goblin, you hope to scare someone. If you put on a costume that makes you look like a mouse, a flower, or a square box, you are trying to fool people and make them believe you are not a human being. If you want to sneak up unseen for a "trick or treat," you might camouflage yourself in gray or black material, or wear a costume that blends in with the outdoor environment, as hunters and soldiers sometimes do. Some insects do this, too. They take on different shapes or colors and often don't look like insects at all.

THE SIX-LEGGED TREE TWIG

(Walking Stick)

If your home is near many trees, in late summer you may find a very odd insect clinging to the screen of a door or window. It is there quite accidentally, perhaps blown out of its usual haunts by the wind or a rain storm. This is your best chance to see it, for if you searched the trees and bushes where it lives you would probably never see it, even if it were right in front of your nose. That's because it looks exactly like a twig or the stem of a leaf. This insect is called a walking stick.

The walking stick has a very long, thin body; long, thin jointed legs; and thin threadlike feelers. Its head is so small that it is hard to tell which end is which. The walking stick's body may be green or

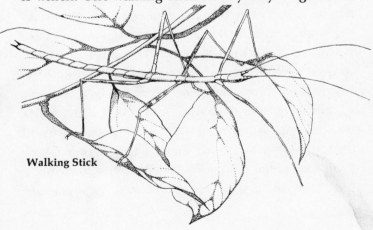

Walking Stick

brown, and it has several rings around it that resemble the growth rings of a leafy twig. It often rests among leaves with its forelegs stretched straight out, and it looks as if it were growing on the tree. The walking stick has no wings.

This insect does not go through any startling external changes during its lifetime. The female drops her eggs one by one, in a very haphazard way. They are small, and fall to the ground like seeds. In fact, they even look like seeds! Some will hatch the following spring, and others will lie on the ground for two years before hatching. The young will be quite green at first, like a fresh spring growth. During the summer they will molt five or six times as they grow, and gradually they turn brownish, just as a green twig gradually turns brown.

The walking stick is a good example of mimicry, which is imitating or looking like something else. Why would this be useful to an insect? One good reason is for protection from its enemies. The walking stick cannot fly because it has no wings. It cannot move about rapidly or easily, and it has no way to defend itself. Its best hope for survival is to be overlooked. That may be one reason why it remains so still when it is daylight, almost as if it were in a trance. During the night it is more active and will usually search for food, such as tree leaves. Many birds eat walking sticks when they can find them, but the walking stick has one more trick it can use for escape. It may just drop to the ground, like a dead twig falling from a tree branch.

THORN IN THE SIDE OF A GARDENER

(Buffalo Tree-Hopper)

Many other common insects in our backyards are dressed up to look like parts of the plants they live on. Another one you may find, if your eyes are sharp, is the Buffalo tree-hopper. It's very likely that you will overlook it completely if it is not moving because it looks like a small thorn on the side of a plant stem.

The Buffalo tree-hopper is very oddly shaped,

Buffalo Tree-Hopper

with a large three-sided hump on its back. Its head and body are hardly visible under a huge neck shield. The Buffalo tree-hopper is green, but some other tree-hoppers are brown with spines or strange protuberances on their forebodies. Sometimes they are called the brownies of the insect world because they look like brownies wearing funny hats, if you look at them from the front.

Tree-hoppers are sucking insects. They may cause considerable damage to plants and trees because they lay their eggs in growing plants. Sometimes these eggs are carefully placed in parallel rows in stems or twigs. The eggs are not crushed because the slits the females make slow down or stunt the growth of the plant between the rows.

Although the tree-hoppers may look like parts of a plant to you or me, scientists are not sure whether they fool all their natural enemies this way. After all, many hunt by smell rather than sight. And what looks like a thorn to us may not appear to be a thorn to other creatures.

INSECT OR SOAPSUDS?

(Froghopper)

Early in the summer when you walk through a grassy field or along a roadside, you will find bits of foam on many plant stems. They look like tiny masses of soapsuds. There is a tiny insect, well concealed and well protected, under all the foam. Some are so tiny, sometimes less than one-tenth of an inch in size, that you will have trouble finding them in the bubbles. How strange to spend part of your life masquerading as a mass of bubbles! In fact, this insect fooled people for a long time. One of its common names is froghopper. This comes from the early belief that frogs made these masses of foam. It is also called a spittlebug.

The young froghoppers, or spittlebugs, build these odd foam coverings and live underneath them. They feed by sucking the juices of a plant through their beaks. The mass of foam is made from the excess sap that the froghopper has sucked from the plant. As it grows, it makes bigger masses of foam that last for hours or days.

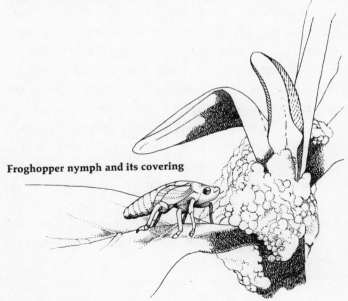

Froghopper nymph and its covering

The foamy bubbles have numerous purposes. They serve as protection from enemies. They also shield it from the direct rays of the sun and provide a rather crude kind of air conditioning.

The froghopper only spends part of its life in this foam shelter. Underneath it grows and molts. During the last molt it develops wings; then it flies away. It may not travel a great distance, for the adult prefers to hop from plant to plant rather than to fly about. The female lays her eggs in the stems of plants, and they will hatch out the following spring.

A SHEEP IN WOLF'S CLOTHING

(Bee Fly)

Another very good way to protect yourself from your enemies is to dress up like a very dangerous creature, even if underneath you are quite harmless. Many insects do this. On a warm sunny day you may find one. It is a fuzzy creature that flies close to the ground and visits various flowers. At first you think it is a small bee because its furry covering is often yellow and black, and it has a long proboscis that resembles a bee's stinger. However, it isn't a bee because it cannot sting and only sucks nectar from flowers. Actually, it is a fly and is called a bee fly because of its appearance and its actions. Like a bee, it is a fast flier. And when it is caught, it will buzz like a bee.

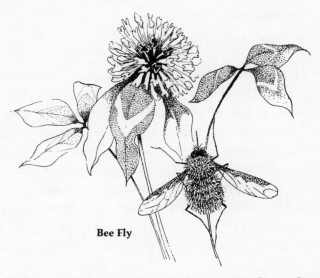

Bee Fly

How can you be sure that this is a fly and not a bee? The real giveaway is the number of wings. A true fly has only one pair of wings, and a bee has two pairs.

Some kinds of bee flies associate with true bees, although the end result of this association is tragic for the bees. The bee flies hover around the nests of wild bees and deposit their very small eggs at the entrance. The eggs hatch out into tiny, spiny maggots. These maggots work their way down into the bees' nest and into the cells where the bee larvae are sealed up. There they remain to suck on the bee larvae and eventually kill them. The larvae of other species of bee flies prey upon the eggs and larvae of grasshoppers, wasps, and beetles.

THE BIRD THAT ISN'T

(Sphinx Moth)

Have you ever watched a hummingbird hovering over a flower bed, thrusting his long beak down into the petals of petunias or honeysuckle? Next time look again, carefully. It may not be a hummingbird at all, but it may be a sphinx moth. The moth is almost the same size as the bird. Its wings beat very rapidly, just as the hummingbird's wings do. When the moth pauses in midair, uncurls its tongue which is longer than its body, and dips it into a blossom to siphon off nectar, it is easily mistaken for a bird.

The moth's resemblance to a hummingbird is not really a masquerade, for the resemblance is just coincidental. However, at one time during its life cycle it does manage to wear a frightful costume to bluff its enemies.

Sometimes adult sphinx moths are called hawk-moths. They are large insects, and their wings may measure four inches from tip to tip. The wings are rather narrow and grayish in color, not as colorful as many other moths. Their bodies are thick and pointed at both ends. They can fly about swiftly and are most active at dusk. During the day they are quiet, as if napping, with their forelegs over their eyes, their antennae folded under their wings, and their long tongues tightly curled under their heads, like a watch spring.

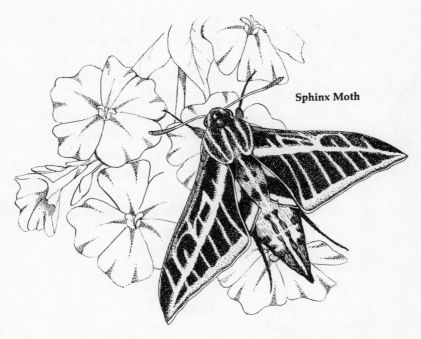

Sphinx Moth

The female hawkmoth of one species lays her eggs on tomato or tobacco plants. The eggs look like little seed pearls. In about a week the baby caterpillars, known as hornworms, gnaw holes in the eggs and crawl out. They grow rapidly, until they are about three inches long. At this time they can eat as much as two plant leaves a day. They are bright green with diagonal markings on their bodies. Near the end of their bodies is a hornlike structure. It looks like it might be poisonous but it is harmless, perhaps even useless, for scientists have not discovered the reason for the structure.

When the hornworm is disturbed, it rears up in

a menacing way and holds the forepart of its body rigid. This apparently looked like the pose of a sphinx to someone, sometime, for that is supposedly the origin of the name sphinx moth. The pose is all bluff, for it has no way to protect itself.

Although the tomato hornworm is large and conspicuous when it is nearly fullgrown, you may find one you will not recognize. It may have dozens of small ovals, like tiny white footballs, on its back. These are actually the cocoons of a wasp which has laid its eggs in the living caterpillar. The wasp larvae feed on the body of the caterpillar.

At the end of the summer, the hornworm burrows a short distance into the ground and pupates. Now it is encased in a hard, brown covering and resembles a brown jug with a handle. The "handle" contains the proboscis that is arched away from its body.

In the spring the hawkmoth will emerge from the pupal case, climb onto a twig, and rest while the wings expand. During this time it must also fit together the two grooved halves of its long tongue so that it can set about the business of sucking nectar from flowers.

HIDE AND SEEK

Many insects are very strange looking to begin with, so it is most confusing when they look like something else. Why have insects developed these odd masquerades and resemblances to other things? The main reason is for protection.

It usually takes thousands of years and many, many generations for any creature to develop a specialized pattern of color, marking, or shape for protection. But there is one moth, called the peppered moth, found in England that did this trick in about 50 years. Its favorite resting place was on a lichen-covered tree trunk; its light-colored, speckled wings blended perfectly with this background. But then smoke and soot from industry began to darken the tree trunks, and the moth showed up very plainly against the dark bark. Then a blackish-colored form of this same moth began to appear in large numbers, and the lighter ones almost disappeared. The English people became concerned about the soot and smoke that were polluting the air and passed laws to control it. Gradually the trees became cleaner and lighter, and once again that moth was too conspicuous. Now more of the lighter-colored moths are becoming prevalent, which is evidence that they once again are changing their appearance to suit the environment.

Some caterpillars, such as the tomato hornworm and the polyphemus moth larvae, are as green as the leaves they feed upon. The markings may even resemble lines of sunlight and shadow through leaves.

Perhaps you have seen pictures of soldiers in a jungle that have tucked leaves and short branches in their helmets so that they will blend into their surroundings. Some insects, such as the larvae of some lacewing flies, carry bits of foliage or other debris around on their backs or heads, too.

Camouflaged insects may be overlooked by enemies, such as birds that are searching for tasty morsels. But many insects are hunters themselves, lying in wait for their prey. Some of these, too, are colored in such a way that they are not easily seen, such as the praying mantis.

Color can also be used as a warning or bluffing device. There are insects that are very drab in color and hard to see when at rest, but if they are disturbed, they can flash a bright color that may startle or frighten an enemy. Strange markings or spots may help to repel unfriendly visitors. The big eye spots on some of the click beetles, or the extra "eyes" on some caterpillars are examples.

"Now you see me, now you don't" is another kind of protective coloration. Many moths are very bright, even gaudy when they are flying, but they seem to drop out of sight when they alight and fold their brilliant wings in such a way that the color does not show. Some grasshoppers have colorful flying wings, but they tuck these under dun-colored wing covers at rest.

The most unusual masquerades are those that are assumed by some insects so that they closely resemble another. One of the best and most common examples you can find is a monarch butterfly and his mimic, the viceroy. The viceroy is smaller than the monarch, but the coloring is almost exactly the same, and the wing markings are so similar that you have to look very closely to see the difference. Few birds would take the time to find out which is which. And that is the reason for this close resemblance. The monarch butterfly is not a food that birds relish, for apparently it is distasteful to them. The viceroy, on the other hand, may have a very good flavor, but experienced birds are not likely to take a chance on that. Thus the viceroy is protected because it looks like a bad-tasting relative.

The viceroy spends a good portion of its life as a copycat. Only the adult resembles the monarch. The larva is most unattractive and looks like a bird dropping. The chrysalis is not jade green, like the monarch's, but looks like a dead willow leaf. Only when it emerges with wings does it have this startling likeness to a monarch.

Some harmless insects that lack any means of protecting themselves dress up like others that are more dangerous, such as the bee fly. Great horns, such as those on the stag beetle, or extra spines, such as on some caterpillars, are not useful for protection but look like they might be.

In the insect world the game of hide-and-seek takes on many forms, but it is a deadly game of life and death.

7

Backyard Oddities

SOME OF the common inhabitants of the small-scale insect world are interesting simply because of their odd shapes, peculiar habits, or brilliant colors. The remarkable and often fantastic variations are the result of slow evolution and modifications as insects adapted to many different environmental conditions. Some that evolved were not successful and became extinct; they are known now only as fossils. Others are so strange that it seems as if they were intended as a joke.

136

THE BUG WITH A WHEEL

(Assassin Bug)

The assassin bug is one of these oddities. Be careful when observing this insect. Since it has a painful bite, it is best not to handle it.

The kind you are most likely to find is known as the wheel bug. It is about one inch long and dark brown or black. In the middle of its back is a semi-circular crest that sticks up as if it had part of a cogwheel growing from its body. There doesn't seem to be any good reason for this, but it does make it easy to identify. Its head is so long and narrow that it appears to have a neck. It really doesn't have one, because no insect has a neck.

The assassin bug is a hunter, and it seeks out caterpillars, beetles, and cockroaches. It will seize a victim with its front legs, insert its powerful beak

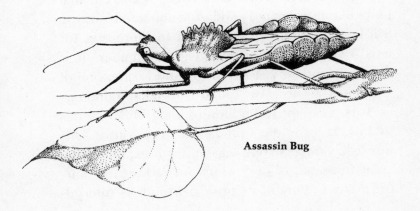

Assassin Bug

into the victim, and suck out the juices. The beak is carried in a sheath under the bug's head, like a tiny sword in a scabbard. When the assassin bug is disturbed, it squeaks by rubbing the tip of its beak against ridges in the groove in which the beak is held.

The female wheel bug lays her eggs in a six-sided design on the bark of trees and bushes. The eggs look like black bottles with white stoppers. The nymphs, when they hatch out, have "buttons" on their backs which develop into the "cogwheel" they carry about.

HANDSOME IS AS HANDSOME DOES

(Fiery Searcher Ground Beetle)

Undoubtedly there is a large beetle in your backyard that is a truly handsome creature. It is a shiny blue-green iridescent color, edged with red, that looks like an animated jewel. And animated it is; you will have to be fast on your feet to capture it, for it is a very swift runner and good climber. It is known as the fiery searcher ground beetle, one of a group that are also called caterpillar hunters.

It is most apt to be found hiding under stones or lurking near the foundation of a house. This insect has long, strong legs and will explore large areas in search of prey which it captures in a surprise attack. One of its principal foods is caterpil-

Fiery Searcher Ground Beetle

lars, and it will climb trees and bushes to get them. It is particularly useful to man because it feeds greedily on the destructive gypsy moth caterpillars and tent caterpillars.

What causes the shiny, metallic sheen of this beetle and the coloration of other insects? The source of all color is light, and the color we see is determined by which wave lengths or rays of the light are reflected to our eyes by the surface the light strikes. Some colors are the result of pigments which absorb all the rays except one; a red cloth, for example, reflects only the red rays and absorbs all others. Most of the bright hues that insects have are due to pigments in the cells of the outer body wall. Such colors as red, yellow, and brown often come from chemicals in the foods the insects eat, from body wastes, or from enzyme action in the body. The green of some caterpillars comes from the chlorophyll of the foliage they feed on, for example.

The shiny, iridescent colors of some insects, such as the fiery searcher ground beetle and other animals are known as structural colors. The light rays hit the surface of the insect's body or wings, and the light is refracted or broken up by the structure of the surface tissues, much as a prism separates white light into a rainbow. These colors do not fade as readily as pigment colors when the creature dies because the tissues are fully formed and do not change as much as the chemicals that cause pigment colors.

Some insects have both structural and pigment colors. They may even change color in a certain temperature or light intensity. Many change color as they mature. They may appear quite pale immediately after molting, until new coloring is formed. Sometimes insects which emerge late in the season are darker or even quite different in color from the same kind that came out earlier in the summer. Color alone is not a reliable means of identification of an insect, but it is useful.

PLAY BALL!

(Tumblebug)

Beetles, beetles, everywhere! There are so many of them and so many different kinds; you can find them almost any place you look, indoors and outdoors. Whether large or small, you can generally determine whether an insect is a beetle or not by looking at the structure of the wings. There are four wings, and the front pair is thick, and either leathery or hard and brittle. They usually meet straight down the middle of the insect's back, and they aren't suitable for flying about. The front wings protect the back wings which are longer and flexible. When not in use, the back wings fold under the front ones.

Beetles bite or chew their food and have well-developed jaws for this purpose. Many are destructive, but others are more helpful to man by destroying harmful insects or by acting as scavengers.

There's one beetle that is worth searching for just to watch his odd activity. He spends most of his time rolling a ball of dirt around. He is known as a dung beetle, or tumblebug. One of the best places to find him is in a pasture.

The tumblebug collects animal wastes, usually that of cattle. He presses it into a ball with his four hind legs, and then spins and turns it around until it is hard and round. Now he grasps it firmly with his two hind legs, plants his middle and front legs firmly on the ground and starts to push the ball backwards. Sometimes two tumblebugs roll a ball around together, one pushing and the other pulling. They may roll their ball a great distance before they bury it.

A really choice ball may cause a tumblebug bat-

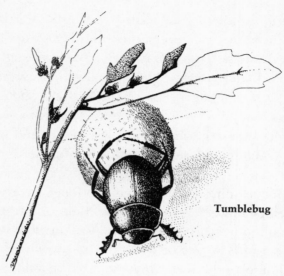

Tumblebug

tle. Another dung beetle may try to steal the ball away from its owner, and a short fight may take place. This seldom amounts to very much, and the loser may end up helping to roll the ball around.

The ball of dung is both food for the adult tumblebug and a nursery for the young. The female lays an egg inside a buried dung ball. The egg is protected, and when the larva hatches out, it has plenty of food all around.

FLYING TIGER

(Swallowtail Butterfly)

The largest and most colorful butterflies that you are apt to find in your backyard are the swallowtails. You will know them by the long tips that extend from the end of their wings, like tails.

One of the most common is known as the tiger swallowtail. It is bright yellow with black stripes on the front wings and black edgings on the back wings. The black strips on yellow are like those of a tiger, but it certainly is not tigerish in any other way. In some regions, the female swallowtail may be dark brown or black, rather than yellow, and the pattern of stripes is more difficult to see.

Scientists are not certain why some butterflies have long extensions on their wings. One reason may be that the tails are a form of protection. The swallowtail is so big and gaudy that it would seem to be an easy target for a hungry bird. However, the bird that attacks a swallowtail butterfly may strike

Swallowtail Butterfly

at the wing tails and miss the delicate body parts. At night the butterfly sleeps in the grass where it is less conspicuous with its wings brought together above its back.

The adults are primarily flower feeders, as all butterflies are, but the tiger swallowtail larvae eat wild cherries. The female lays her eggs on a wild cherry tree. She may lay as many as 200, but she rarely puts more than one or two on each leaf.

After the larva hatches it is tiny and black with a white saddle. It promptly eats the shell of its egg and then starts munching on the wild cherry leaves. It will shed its skin four times in the next few weeks, and each time the skin pattern changes a little. As it grows, it becomes bright green and develops two big eyelike spots on the side of its head, which are yellow-green edged with black. When it is at rest it expands the forepart of its body; now it looks like the head of a green snake with great staring eyes. This false face is a bit startling, and serves as protection against birds and other insects.

The swallowtail caterpillar has other protective devices, too. Near the front of its head are two orange-colored scent organs. When it is disturbed, the organs protrude and emit a disagreeable odor. At the same time it may weave its forebody about in a menacing way. The big staring eyes, the horns, and the bad smell are enough to make most enemies retreat in haste.

As the period of the swallowtail's life as a caterpillar nears an end, it prepares to form a chrysalis. Its body color gradually changes from bright green to dull brown. It spins a little silk pad and attaches it to a branch or other object. It also makes a safety belt that goes around the middle of its body and holds the chrysalis upright or at an angle. Then it overwinters in this case that looks almost like a chip of wood.

INSECTS ARE WHERE AND WHEN YOU FIND THEM

Early and midsummer are the most active periods for insects. This is when the insects are singing full force, laying eggs, forming cocoons, or seeking hiding places for the approaching cold weather.

The number of insects that may be seen in any one area will vary from season to season, from day to day, and even from hour to hour. Certain insects are no longer as abundant in or near urban areas because their special plant foods, which may be considered weeds by man, have been uprooted or mowed down. But day or night, winter or summer, you can find some of these interesting members of a small-scale world if you are patient and observant.

8

An Insect Zoo

YOU CAN watch the activities of many backyard insects over a period of time by keeping them in suitable containers. You can see all or part of the life cycle of some of the "quick-change artists" or watch their daily living habits close up. A live insect walking or jumping or eating is much more fun than a dead one stuck on a pin.

You will need a net, bottles or boxes, a knife, and perhaps a pair of tweezers to help capture the members for your insect zoo. Make a net out of cheesecloth, mosquito netting, or nylon. First bend a coat hanger into a circle; straighten the hook out and bind it securely to a broom handle or stout stick. Cut the material into a triangular shape, fold it in half, and stitch a long seam down one side. Fasten the open end of this cloth to the wire rim with coarse thread by lapping the edge of the material over the wire and stitching round and round. Be sure the cone is long enough so that it can be flipped over the net's opening or around the handle to prevent the captured insect from escaping.

You can use this net to scoop insects out of the air or from the plants. Chasing a lively butterfly or moth across the lawn may be fun, but it is often a waste of time. Instead, try to catch it as it is feeding. Watch your insect a while, and then lie in wait near its favorite feeding station. Most insects fly or hop straight up when they are disturbed; so come down from the top or take a side sweep.

There are other devices for capturing insects, too. You can use a net and sweep through the grass or low limbs of trees and bushes to bag quite a variety of creatures. You may need a stouter net for this, made of canvas with the wire rim securely attached to the handle.

A large wire kitchen sieve or a mesh tea strainer will serve as a water net. Scoop this along the bottom of a pond or stream, or let the current flow directly into it. You can also collect many insects that live around water by pulling up weeds and pond plants.

At night you can hold a square of heavy cardboard or a canvas frame under the limbs of trees and bushs. Beat the branches and collect sleepy specimens as they drop down.

Many times you can simply pop a wide-mouthed jar over the unsuspecting insect you want.

Handle the insects carefully, preferably with tweezers. Never hold an insect by its wings or legs; grasp it by the body. The best way is to "cage" it immediately by sliding a bottle into the net, rather than transferring it by hand.

One word of caution, if you want to watch live insects, you will have to give them a little care from time to time. You cannot just put them into a jar and forget them.

You can set up an insect zoo in many kinds of cages and containers. You can use:

1. A wide-mouthed jar or a discarded fish bowl. Stretch a piece of gauze or window screening around the top and secure it with a string or

This is one type of "cage" you can have in your zoo.

twist of wire. Some insects will prefer a layer of soil on the bottom.

2. A shoe box. Cut the bottom out of the box, and cut out a section of the lid. Cover the openings with heavy plastic or cellophane, taped securely along the sides. Fasten the lid shut with strong rubber bands, and stand the box upright.

3. A glass cage. This can be made from three oblong pieces of glass that are the same shape, and two square pieces for the ends. Fit the glass sides together inside and out with strips of adhesive tape, and make a mesh or wire lid for the top.

4. A frame cage. A sturdier cage can be made by fitting pieces of glass into a wooden frame, or by stretching a wire lid over an old oblong glass aquarium. A wooden frame can be covered with window screening, too. Screening is sometimes difficult to see through, so heavy plastic or a sheet of glass can be used for one or two sides. You can use an old piece of rubber from an inner tube for the top. Tack it on all four edges, then slit a line through the center. You will be able to put your hand in this crack to add specimens or food, but the insects won't be able to jump or crawl out.

Insects do not need a great deal of oxygen. It is not necessary to punch a lot of holes in the lid of a bottle as most people do. Proper ventilation is necessary to prevent the air from getting musty and to prevent mold from forming on food or soil. Gauze or screening will permit the air to circulate.

As we have seen, some insects are vegetarians and others are meat eaters. The vegetarians are usually found on their favorite plant food. You can cut a supply when you capture them. If they are not eating when you catch them, you may have to experiment to find out what they like to eat.

Leaves or grass must be kept fresh and renewed frequently. One good way to keep them fresh is to cut off stalks or twigs of a plant and stand the ends in a small jar or a pot of wet sand. Be sure there is no standing water because most insects will drown in less than a teaspoon of liquid. Many will like bits of lettuce, fresh fruit, or vegetables parings.

The meat eaters are more of a problem, for you will have to do the hunting for them. Meal worms which you can buy at a pet supply store or a dot of raw hamburger will do for some if you cannot find enough live spiders and insects for their meals.

Water is essential for all insects, but it must be supplied sparingly. Sprinkle a bit over the leaves or ground, or even over the top of the cage. Many insects will get enough from the plants they feed on if the stalks are fresh and juicy.

INTERESTING INMATES

You can make your own aphid battlefield in a glass jar or cardboard box by cutting a branch of the rosebush or other plant where you can find numerous aphids. Set the stalks in water or damp sand to keep the plants fresh. Make sure there is cotton or paper tucked around the base of the stalks to prevent the insects from falling into the water. Now you may add aphid enemies as you find them, such as ladybugs, ladybird larvae, and aphis-lions. With a little luck you may be able to watch the whole life cycle of a lacewing fly by adding a plant stalk which has some of the lacewing fly eggs on it.

Cut off the branch or leaf on which you have found a ladybird pupa and add that. In a day or so you will have a grown-up ladybird. Tuck in a fresh stalk for food now and then, and keep your magnifying glass handy.

An ant nest will be a good addition to your insect zoo. A glass jar filled one-half full of earth is a simple way to keep them.

A simple house can be provided in a flat pan, although you cannot watch what goes on underground. Fill a shallow pan with soil, and cover half of it with a sheet of glass. Set this pan into a larger pan of water. The water forms a moat around the edge that keeps the ants from escaping. Put your captured colony into a depression in the dirt. Later you can set a branch covered with aphids into the soil, and watch the ants milk them.

A glass house sandwich can be constructed by fitting two pieces of glass that are about sixteen inches square into groves made in two blocks of wood that measure about fifteen inches long, two inches wide, and one inch thick. The two grooves need to be cut about one inch apart down the long side of each block. Then the two wooden pieces, with the grooves facing inward, need to be attached to a third piece of wood that is the same size. This third piece of wood forms the base for the glass sandwich. After the two pieces of glass are put in the grooves, fill the sandwich about two-thirds full of porous soil. Then put a strip of wood across the top, and either tape or hinge it so it can be lifted up when adding food. Air holes should be made and covered with wire screen.

Now dig up an ant hill, taking good care to secure a queen ant. Carry your colony home in a paper sack or plastic bag. With a paper funnel, pour the contents of the sack into the ant house. Set the house in a dark place for a day or so. This will give the ants a chance to adjust to their new home.

Feed ants by putting one or two drops of honey, corn syrup, or molasses into their house with a medicine dropper. Add a bit of apple, raisin, banana, or cake. Dampen the soil very lightly now and then, or keep a small piece of moistened sponge on the surface.

Spiders can be caged, too, but they will insist upon live food. You will have to trap insects and release them in the cage. If you suspend a spider's cocoon of eggs in the cage, you can watch the spiderlings emerge.

Crickets and grasshoppers make very satisfactory pets and are easy to care for. Capture them before they have wings, if possible, and you can watch them grow by "molts and bounds!" Crickets will like some dirt in the bottom of their cages and some sort of hiding place. A crumpled bit of newspaper, an empty matchbox, or a few rocks will do. Feed them grass, lettuce, bread, small pieces of raw meat, or tiny slices of fresh fruit. Be sure there is some moisture available and plenty of ventilation so that the cage will not become moldy.

Grasshoppers can be fed fresh grass, clover, bits of fruit, and they are very fond of corn silk. A hungry grasshopper will remind you of someone eating an ear of corn when he grasps a blade of greenery and eats along the edge.

Katydids need a diet of maple leaves, oak leaves, lettuce, and fresh fruit, such as apples and cherries. If you are lucky enough to find a "walking stick," it will need plenty of fresh leaves, too.

A praying mantis is a real "conversational piece" pet. Be careful when you pick it up, for the legs break off easily. Grasp the mantis by the back of the head. A few twigs and branches in the insect cage will allow it to be in the environment it needs; but it is docile and slow enough to be allowed to roam about the house exploring if no one in the family objects. It will get quite tame, and learn to drink from a teaspoon and to accept live insects, spiders, or meal worms from a pair of tweezers. A mantis' appetite is tremendous. It will eat grasshoppers, wasps, beetles, and raw meat, but no vegetables. Keep one pet mantis at a time, for they will eat each other. A mantis egg case can be brought into the house in late spring or stored in a cool place. If the mantise hatch before other insects are plentiful, you will have a bit of trouble keeping them fed. If mantise are not easily found in your locality, egg cases can be purchased from a number of supply houses.

Cicadas, click beetles, and bugs are all fun to watch in captivity. If you are uncertain about the proper diet, experiment with leaves, grasses or fruit for these vegetarians. Try a little banana or even a bit of boiled potato. Remember to put in only very small quantities of food, and don't forget to sprinkle water in the cage occasionally.

An ant-lion can be kept in a small pan or a saucer of sand. Once he has dug his own pit, put in a few ants.

Keeping live moths and butterflies is not very satisfactory. However, rearing the larvae and caterpillars will give you an opportunity to see part of their life cycle. You can reduce the feeding problems in your zoo by collecting caterpillars in the middle or late summer when they are large and nearly ready to pupate. Then you may cage them with a few twigs or stalks of the plant upon which they were feeding. When the moth or butterfly has pupated, you may have to wait several weeks or even over the winter to see it emerge.

Store overwintering cocoons and chrysalids in a cool place, and dampen them slightly about once a week or so. They do not need protection from the cold, but must be kept from drying out. When the weather warms up, put the cocoon or chrysalid in a convenient place to watch. Do not hang it on the wall, for the fluid that comes out when the insect emerges may leave a stain that is hard to remove.

A tomato hornworm is a good specimen to start with, for it is easy to find and large enough to watch easily. Put a well-fed caterpillar in a jar with a few tomato leaves and an inch or so of soil in the bottom. One day you will find it burrowing into the soil, looking shriveled and unhealthy. In a short time it will be inactive, encased in its "little brown jug," with the distinctive handle that enfolds the adult sphinx moth's proboscis.

In the fall you will find insects hibernating in many ways—as egg cases, cocoons, chrysalids—and they will be up under the eaves of your house, in or on the ground, on trees, shrubs, and low plants. Carefully remove those that interest you, store them in a box with netting or screening in a cool place. Label them with your best guess as to what they are. In the spring you will know how many you guessed right.

You can add aquariums to your zoo, and stock

them with dragonflies and mosquitoes, as well as numerous water bugs and beetles. A glass jar or an old fish bowl will do very well. Do not worry about clean water because they won't like it. Use water from the pond where you collect your specimens and be sure it is full of decaying plant material and mud. Add a stick that extends above the level of the water. If you can find a female dragonfly depositing eggs, bring the stalk home and set it in your aquarium. In a short time, the nymphs will emerge and become water dwellers where you can watch their strange feeding habits. If you also collect partially grown nymphs, you will have a transformation sooner. This often happens quite early in the morning, so check each day so as not to miss it. Do not overstock a small jar or aquarium with your specimens. And do not put mosquito larvae in the same jar with dragonfly nymphs unless you intend mosquitoes as food.

Indoors or out, you are going to make many discoveries about the insects in your backyard. Some of your adventures will be expected—and others will be unexpected. By close observation you may even uncover some new facts about the inhabitants of the strange, small-scale world because much remains to be discovered.

Index

J
595.7

Edsall
Battle on the rosebush

WITHDRAWN